The Complete KETO DESSERTS Cookbook

AMAZINGLY DELICIOUS LOW-CARB DESSERTS RECIPES FOR THE BUSY PEOPLE ON KETO DIET

Dr Gabrielle J Williams

Table of Contents

Description

We all want that nice delicacy after a meal and if you are looking to live a healthy life by consuming low carb foods, then keto dessert is the best way to go! Keto diet has many health benefits and suits almost everyone especially the person with diabetes.

If you want keto desserts that won't disappoint your family your guests but impress even the diehard carboholics, choose keto desserts. Are you looking for those low carb desserts that best fit a keto diet? This book has the best recipes that fit in perfectly with your macros; these are keto dessert recipes you can trust.

My book focuses on not only satisfying the sweet-tooth but also living a healthy lifestyle while indulging in amazing desserts while on a Keto Diet, I promise you that upon reading my book, you will have all the fundamental information needed to dive into the world of Ketogenic Diet and come out with a healthier physique!

So, what are you waiting for? Don't miss out on your opportunity to get a huge amount of mouthwatering Ketogenic Dessert recipes while learning the tricks and trades of the diet at the same time!

Introduction

With several high-quality scientific research done on Keto diets; the low-carb diets are generally accepted as an effective tool in attaining real weight loss. Your body can be turned into a fat-burning machine whose outcome includes weight loss amongst other benefits. The burning of fat is massively increased, while the fat-storing hormone, insulin levels drop significantly. This generates an ideal situation in the human system, where the fat loss in the body can ensue, without hunger.

Going the keto way, you get to gain better control over your appetite level. Whenever your body burns fat, it gets continuous access to weeks, even months, of stored energy. This process intensely reduces any hunger feelings. It is also a very known experience, as it is also backed up by research. Keto diets are easy to consume less if you plan on losing excess weight alongside super-charged efforts to reversing any type 2 diabetes. Desirably, users get to save more money by not having to take snack regularly. Several individuals only believe it is okay to eat once or even twice a day (skipping breakfast regularly). Having a better appetite control over hunger can potentially be beneficial with issues relating to food addiction or sugar, and maybe some eating disorders as well. At best, the feeling of being satisfied is definitely part of your solution. With it, you can possibly see food as your friend and not an enemy, or simply fuel to whatsoever you desire.

Ketogenic diets can immensely improve your bodily endurance by providing continuous access to all the stored fat energy. The human system supply of glycogen, stored carbohydrates, only lasts for few hours after an intense workout. But your stored fat transmits enough energy to effortlessly last for days, even weeks.

The ketogenic diet is an effective and proven medical therapy for epilepsy. It has been used since the mid-1920s. Conventionally, it was used mainly for kids, but lately, grown-ups have also

Recipes

1. Beef Machaca Keto Muffins

Make these muffins and enjoy them during your breakfast.
Makes: 8 muffins
Prep time: 10 min
Cook time: 30 min
Ingredients
2 tablespoons steak drippings, or the bacon drippings
½ cup of Beef Jerky Machaca
4 organic eggs
½ cup of roasted tomatillo salsa
½ cup of almond flour
Directions
1. Pre-heat the oven up to 350 degrees.
2. In your 7" nonstick ceramic pan placed on a medium heat, just melt fat of choice then add machaca to it.
3. Stir for 3 minutes or for the machaca to soften and fragrant.
4. Allow to cool for about 5 minutes.
5. In food processor, just add eggs, almond flour, tomatillo salsa and machaca.
6. Mix on low for 30 seconds, or until all the ingredients become well blended.
7. Pour the mixture into some 8 silicone muffin cups, or into silicone muffin mold.
8. Bake for 30 minutes at 350 degrees or until the toothpick becomes clean when it has been inserted in to muffin.
   Nutritional information per serving: Calories 128, Fat 10g, Fiber 0.75g, Protein 6.6g

2. Sesame Keto Buns

Make these fat bombs good for you if you on a ketogenic diet.
Makes: 12 buns
Prep time: 15 min
Cook time: 50 min
Ingredients
1 cup of coconut flour
½ cup of sesame seeds and ½ cup for covering the buns
½ cup of pumpkin seeds
½ cup of psyllium powder
1 cup of hot water
1 tbs of Celtic sea salt
1 tbs of baking powder
8 egg whites
Directions
1. Pre-heat your oven up to 350 degrees.
2. Combine all the dry ingredients in the large bowl.
3. Mix well.
4. In some blender, blend egg whites until they are very foamy.
5. Add foamy egg whites to dry ingredients then mix well using a spoon, or in food processor.
6. The dough will still be crumbly.
7. Add 1 cup of the boiling water to mix then keep stirring until the smoother dough forms.
8. The dough will remain to be crumbly but it will stick when formed into bun.
9. Press the buns into the plate where the ½ cup of the sesame seeds was poured, so seeds will stick to top.

10. Place some sheet of the parchment paper on the cookie sheet.
11. Place the buns on paper.
12. Bake for 50 minutes at 350
13. Let cool inside oven for an extra crunchy top.
14. Makes 12 small buns
    Nutritional information per serving: Calories 133, Fat 6.5g, Fiber 9.5g, Protein 6.9g

3. Cookie Dough Fat Bombs

Make these cookie dough fat bombs and get all the essential fats.
Makes: 10 servings
Prep Time: 5 min
Ingredients
1/2 cup of coconut oil, melted
1/4 cup of almond Yum butter or the almond butter
1 tablespoon of maple syrup or some 10 drops of liquid stevia
3/4 cup of almond flour
1/4 cup of dark chocolate, finely chopped
Directions
1. In some bowl, combine almond butter, coconut oil, maple syrup, almond flour then mix well.
2. Fold in the chocolate.
3. Transfer to loaf pan then freeze until set.
4. Cut into squares then store in airtight container kept in the fridge.
   Nutritional information per serving: Calories: 209, Fat: 19.9 g, Unsaturated fat: 9g, Saturated fat: 10.9 g, Trans fat: 0 g, Sugar: 3.7 g, Carbohydrates: 6.7 g, Sodium: 4 mg Fiber: 1.3 g, Cholesterol: 1 mg, Protein: 3.4 g

4. Bacon Wrapped Mozzarella Sticks

Try this recipe and get the best sticks for your breakfast.
Makes: 2 servings
Prep time: 10 min
Cook time: 3 min
Ingredients
1 Frigo of cheese heads cheese stick, mozzarella
2 slices bacon
Coconut oil
Low sugar pizza sauce(optional)
Toothpicks
Directions
1. Preheat the coconut oil in deep fryer up to 350 degrees.
2. Wrap your cut into half cheese sticks and bacon, while overlapping them.
3. Drop the bacon already wrapped with cheese in hot oil then cook until bacon becomes quite brown.
4. Remove to paper towel so as to cool for few minutes. Remove toothpick then enjoy with favorite dipping sauce!
   Nutritional information per serving: Calories: 103, Fat: 9g, Carbohydrates: 1G, Fiber: 0g, Protein: 7g

5. Breakfast Bacon Fat Bombs

Make these bacon fat bombs and enjoy them during your breakfast.
Makes: 6 servings
Prep time: 30 min

Cook Time: 20 min
Ingredients
1 Large Hardboiled Egg
¼ Avocado
4 tbsps. of Unsalted or Clarified Butter
1 tbsp. of Mayonnaise
1 seeded and diced Serrano Pepper
1 tbsp. of Cilantro, chopped
Kosher Salt
Cracked Pepper
Juice of ¼ Lime
2 tbsps. of Bacon Grease
6 Bacon Slices, Cooked
Directions

1. In some large bowl, combine avocado, butter, hardboiled egg, mayonnaise cilantro and serrano pepper. Mash into smooth paste using a fork or a potato smasher. Season using salt and pepper, and add lime juice and stir.
2. Prepare the bacon in favorite fashion until it becomes crispy, while reserving 2 tablespoons bacon grease. Add bacon grease to fat bomb mixture then stir gently. Cover then place in a fridge for about 30 minutes, or until your mixture is cooled and can be formed into solid balls. Crumble bacon into some small bits in some small bowl.
3. Use a spoon to scoop out 6 amounts of fat bomb mixture then form into balls. Just add balls to bacon bits then roll around until they are completely covered.
4. Serve immediately.
Nutritional information per serving: Calories: 103, Fat: 9g, Carbohydrates: 1G, Fiber: 0g, Protein: 7g

6. Cheese, Jalapeno and Bacon Bite Fat Bombs

Make these savory fat bombs and increase your intake for healthy fats.
Makes: 20 servings
Prep Time: 20 min
Cook Time: 20 min
Ingredients
8 ounces of full fat cream cheese or the dripped yogurt cheese
4 slices of chopped and cooked bacon, grease reserved
4 ounces of shredded cheddar cheese
4 jalapeno peppers
3 ounces of coconut oil, expeller-pressed
2 ounces of bacon grease
Directions

1. Melt coconut oil in case it is a solid.
2. Cook the bacon over medium heat and in medium skillet.
3. Dice the Jalapeno peppers after removal of stems then rinsing out the seeds.
4. Combine the cheddar cheese, cream cheese, bacon grease, diced Jalapeno and melted coconut oil.
5. Press the cream cheese mixture to parchment-lined loaf pan then chill for about 2-3 hours.
6. Set the bacon pieces aside.
7. Once the cream cheese mixture has become firm, remove from the loaf pan then cut into 18 pieces.
8. Gently roll them into balls then roll the balls into the crumbled bacon as you desire.
9. Enjoy immediately or keep before you can cover in the bacon in a fridge for about 5 days or in a freezer for about 4 weeks.

Nutritional information per serving: Calories 134, Saturated fat. 9 g, Fat 13 g, Trans fat: 0 g, Sugar: 1 g, Sodium: 107 mg, Carbohydrates: 1 g, Fiber: 0 g, Protein: 3 g

7. Strawberry Cheesecake Fat Bombs

Make these fat bombs and get a high-fat treat.
Makes: 12 servings
Prep time: 5 min
Cook Time: 5 min
Ingredients
6 ounces of full fat cream cheese or a homemade yogurt cheese
2.5 ounces of butter, softened
6 strawberries
¼ teaspoon of vanilla extract
1-1/2 ounce of melted coconut oil
3 packets of Stevia
⅛ Teaspoons of sea salt
Pretty flower candy mold, optional
Directions

1. In your food processor combine the ingredients then puree until smooth.
2. Use some rubber spatula so as to spread the strawberry mixture into the candy mold.
3. Freeze for about 1 hour, then cut in 12 pieces if you are using loaf pan. Continue to freeze until it becomes solid, for another 1-2 hours.
4. Pop out of the candy mold or a loaf pan then store in covered container in a freezer.
5. Allow to thaw for 15 minutes before you can eat for a better taste.
   Nutritional information per serving: Calories: 110, Saturated fat: 8 g, Fat: 11 g, Trans fat: 0 g, Sugar: 1 g, Carbohydrates: 1 g, Sodium: 86 mg, Protein: 1 g, Fiber: 0 g, Cholesterol: 13 mg

8. Nutbutter Cup Fat Bombs

Try this recipe which will give you healthy fats for your healing.
Makes: 12 servings
Prep Time: 5 min
Cook Time: 5 min
Ingredients
½ cup of thick nutbutter
½ cup of softened butter or coconut oil
2 packets of stevia, or 2 tablespoons of honey
½ teaspoon of unrefined sea salt
Directions

1. If the nutbutter has been separated, ensure you mix oil in well or fat bombs will become too soft.
2. Combine the nutbutter, the softened butter or the coconut oil, stevia or the honey, and the sea salt in some small bowl using a fork, or in a food processor with a circular blade.
3. If you are using silicone candy mold, place the mold on some tray or a large plate to transfer it to freezer easily after filling.
4. Once it has been combined, pour this into silicone candy mold or parchment-lined loaf pan or a small casserole dish.
5. Freeze for about 1 hour or until it becomes firm but not solid, then cut in 12 pieces.
6. Store in a freezer, covered then enjoy as desired!
   Nutritional information per serving: Calories: 127, Saturated fat: 5, Fat: 13, Trans fat: 0, Sugar: 1, Sodium: 160 mg, Carbohydrates: 2, Fiber: 1, Cholesterol: 20 mg, Protein: 2

9. Cream Cheese Crab Dip

Make this delicious fat bomb and your family will enjoy it.
Makes: 12 servings
Prep Time 5 min
Cook Time 30 min
Ingredients
8 ounces of lump crab meat
8 ounces of cream cheese softened
1/2 cup of avocado mayonnaise
1 tablespoon of lemon juice
1 teaspoon of Worcestershire sauce
1/2 teaspoon of garlic powder
1/2 teaspoon of onion powder
1/2 teaspoon of salt
1/4 teaspoon of dry mustard
1/4 teaspoon of black pepper
Directions
1. Combine all the ingredients into some small baking dish then spread out evenly.
2. Bake them at 375°F for about 25-30 minutes.
3. Enjoy with a low carb crackers or some vegetables.
   Nutritional information per serving: Calories 142, Total Fat 14.8G, Cholesterol 35mg, Protein 4.2G

10. Flourless Paleo Keto Bomb

Make these low carb fat bombs and enjoy the chocolate taste.
Makes: 16 servings
Prep Time 10 min
Cook Time 25 min
Ingredients
1/2 cup of coconut oil
8 ounces of unsweetened baking chocolate
3 large eggs or some 2 duck eggs kept at room temp
1 1/4 teaspoon of Sweetleaf stevia drops
1 1/4 teaspoon of monk fruit liquid extract
2 teaspoons of vanilla extract
1/4 cup of unsweetened cocoa
1 tablespoon of psyllium husks
1/4 teaspoon of salt preferably sea salt
Directions
1. Place the coconut oil and the unsweetened baking chocolate in some microwaveable bowl. Just microwave these until completely melted.
2. Add stevia, monk fruit, eggs, and vanilla extract to the melted chocolate mixture then combine with the electric mixer.
3. Stir in the unsweetened psyllium husks, cocoa and salt.
4. Spread into a parchment paper lined on a 8x8 baking pan.
5. Bake these at 350°F for about 25 minutes then cool completely before you can slice.
   Nutritional information per serving: Calories 140, Total Fats 15.3G, Cholesterol 15.3Mg, Total Carbs 5g, Protein 3.3g

11. Maple & Pecan Fudge Fat Bombs

These are easy-to-make fat bombs and good for you to enjoy with your family.

Makes: 16 servings

Prep Time: 2 hours
Ingredients
Spiced Maple & Pecan Butter:
3 cups of pecans or walnuts
½ tsp of vanilla powder or 1 tsp of vanilla extract
1 tsp of sugar-free maple extract
Pinch salt
Maple & Pecan Fudge:
1 recipe of Maple & Pecan Butter
¼ cup of powdered Erythritol or a Swerve
½ cup of unsalted butter or a coconut oil
1 ¼ cup of chopped pecans plus 16 pecan halves
10-20 drops of liquid stevia
Directions

1. Start by making Spiced Maple and Pecan Butter. In your food processor, combine pecans, vanilla, maple extract, cinnamon, and salt.
2. Process until they are smooth for some few minutes. Use spatula to scrape your mixture from sides if needed.
3. Add the Erythritol and the butter.
4. Pulse until smooth.
5. Transfer your dough to 8 x 8-inch parchment-lined pan, or some silicone pan. By use of a spatula, spread dough evenly into pan.
6. Add some roughly chopped pecans then mix in.
7. Top with the rest of pecan halves. Refrigerate them for about 1 to 2 hours.
8. Be sure your fudge has been set before you can slice. Keep refrigerated for about 1 week or just freeze for about 3 months.
   Nutritional information per serving: Total carbs 4.2G, Fiber 2.8G, Protein 2.6g, Fat 26G

12. Spinach Coffee Latte

Make Popeye proud, and give it a try! It's actually quite tasty.
Serves 2
Prep time: 3 minutes
Ingredients
1 cup brewed coffee, strong
3/4 cup coconut milk
1/2 cup pumpkin puree
2 handfuls spinach
2 tbsps. butter 1/4
tsp cardamom 2
tbsp erythritol
1/2 tsp vanilla extract
1/2 tsp cinnamon
1/4 tsp allspice
10 drops liquid stevia
1/4 tsp ginger
2 handfuls of ice
Optional: 1/4 cup whisky, bourbon, or scotch
Directions

1. Put all of the wet ingredients and spinach into a very string blender. Blend until the spinach fibers are dissolved (you can also use pre-prepared cubes of the frozen spinach).
2. When the right consistency is achieved, add dry ingredients as well. If you want an alcohol version add liquor at this point.
3. If you want, you can add whipped cream with the dash of cinnamon.

Nutritional Value per serving
Net carbs: 3g, Fat: 13G, Protein: 2.5g, Calories: 154

13. Berry Smoothie

This remarkable drink is so easy to make, but it is going to keep you satisfied for a long time.
Serves 1
Prep time: 3 minutes
Ingredients
⅓ Cup creamed coconut milk or heavy whipping cream
1 tbsp MCT oil or virgin coconut oil
½ cup ice or more
½ cup mixed berries, frozen
½ cup water or almond milk
Optional
3-5 drops stevia extract
½ tsp sugar-free vanilla extract
Whipped cream or coconut milk on top
Directions
1. Take the coconut milk out of the fridge, to a room temperature and let it sit there overnight. Next day, remove liquids (that should be half of the portion).
2. Put the almond and coconut milk together with berries and water into the blender and start mixing. Add MCT oil and if you like more sugary taste add stevia and vanilla as well.
3. Blend everything until nicely combined. Serve immediately and if you want add whipped cream.

Nutritional Value per serving
Net carbs: 7g, Fat: 41G, Fiber: 3.6g, Protein: 4g, Calories: 400

14. Coconut Yogurt

People usually think that it is very complicated to make your own yogurt, but that is not the case. After this easy procedure, you'll get the tastiest and richest yogurt you ever tried.
Serves 2
Prep time: 12-24 hours
Ingredients
1 jar coconut milk, must be full fat
2 capsules of any probiotic
2/3 cup heavy whipping cream
1/2 tsp xanthan gum (1/4 tsp for each of the jars)
Directions
1. Open the coconut milk and stir it well, so that it is well combined. Pour the liquid into 2 large containers.
2. Open capsules of probiotic and add each of them to one container.
3. Put the containers in the oven, under the oven light without opening the oven for 12-24 hours. The liquid gets thicker the longer it stays under the light.
4. When it's, done, put the containers in the fridge to cool down and then into the mixing bowl. Add ½ teaspoon of xantan gum and blend the yogurt with hand mixer to thicken it.
5. In another bowl mix whipping cream until solid. Add heavy whipping cream to yogurt and mix on low. Serve in the smoothie jars and decorate with berries, herbs or cinnamon.

Nutritional Value per serving
Net carbs: 4.3g, Fat: 31.3G, Protein: 0g, Calories: 313

15. Chai Latte

Just wrap your hands around the cup of this spicy drink and it will keep your heart warm.

Serves 2
Prep time: 30 minutes
Ingredients
For Chai mixture
¼ tsp allspice
½ tsp cinnamon
¼ tsp nutmeg
¼ tsp cloves
¼ tsp ginger powder
¼ tsp fennel seeds
4 cardamom pods
2 black tea bags
1 vanilla bean or ½ tsp vanilla powder
¼ tsp salt
2-3 cups water
For base drink
½ cup almond milk
1 tbsp erythritol or swerve
½ cup coconut milk (heavy whipping cream can do as well)
Optional: 10-15 drops stevia extract
Directions
1. Make your chai mixture by putting all of the required spices into a tea bag or you can put them directly into the boiling water. If you decided to use bags, place them into water.
2. Also add bags of black tea into the boiling water, and let it simmer for 20-25 minutes. Remove all of the tea bags and strain the water.
3. In a pan, heat the coconut and almond milk, stir and then pour in the glass. Add the chai mixture to the milk mixture, mix nicely, so that the spices are nicely spread. You should drink it while hot, but it can also be stored in the fridge, and warmed up later.
Nutritional Value per serving
Net carbs: 3.6g, Fat: 13g, Protein: 1.6G, Calories: 132

16. Cheesecake & Berry Smoothie
This is a truly wonderfully looking glass with the prettiest shades of violet that is going to help you stay fit and healthy.
Serves 1
Prep time: 5 minutes
Ingredients
¼ cup full-fat cream cheese (also can be done with creamed coconut milk)
½ cup blackberries
¼ cup heavy whipping cream
1 tbsp MCT oil
½ cup water
½ tsp vanilla extract
Optional: 3-5 drops liquid Stevia
Directions
1. Put cream cheese and heavy cream and blend them until smooth.
2. When combined add MCT oil, water and vanilla. If you want your smoothie to have sweeter taste, add couple of drops of stevia.
3. Add blackberries; blend until very smooth and creamy. Pour in a glass and enjoy.
Nutritional Value per serving
Net carbs: 6.7g, Fat: 53g, Fiber: 4.1G, Protein: 6.4g, Calories: 515

17. Keto Horchata

Creamy and rich keto-friendly version of Mexican classic made only with almonds.

Serves 2

Prep time: 20

Ingredients

2 handfuls almonds blanched
1 cup almond milk, unsweetened
1 large egg
2 tbsps. chia seeds
1 tbsp. lime zest
1 tsp cinnamon (+ 1 WHOLE cinnamon stick)
3 tbsps. erythritol or other low-carb sweeteners
15-20 drops liquid stevia
2 cups warm water

Directions

1. Bleach the almonds and put them with cinnamon stick, lime zest and warm water in a bowl and cover it. Let the liquid rest like that for overnight.
2. After the almonds are soaked, remove the zest and cinnamon, and put the water with almonds into a bowl. Add the almond milk and mix it with hand mixer until nicely combined then place the mixture into a sauce pan, place it on a stove and cook it until it starts sizzling.
3. When it starts to sizzle, add sweeteners and cinnamon. Cook it for two more minutes while stirring.
4. When you take it off the stove, add chia seeds. If you do not like whole chia seeds, grain them. Wait for it to thicken, pour and drink.

Nutritional Value per serving

Net carbs: 5, Fat: 22.2g, Protein: 11.9G, Calories: 282

18. Iced Green Tea

Health benefits of green tea are well known, and now we are giving the version of this drink made for people who what rich flavor and texture and who have exquisite taste.

Serves 1

Prep time: 12 hours

Ingredients

2-3 teabags green tea
1 tbsp. heavy cream
2 tbsps. coconut oil
2 tbsps. butter
3 cups ice cubes

Directions

1. Boil water and after it boils, let it rest for 20 minutes. The water temperature should be about 150F -170F.
2. Place the teabags in the water and, depending on how strong you want it to be, let them sit there for 2-4 minutes before removing them.
3. Add coconut oil, butter and heavy cream and mix it well. It should be well combined, with small bubbles.
4. Place the liquid in a fridge to stay there overnight.
5. Before serving, blend the tea liquid with ice cubes for 3-5 minutes.

Nutritional Value per serving

Net carbs: 0.5g, Fat: 28.5g, Protein: 0g, Calories: 247

BUTTERCREAM

One word for this dessert, heavenly! The combination of butter and soy sauce gives this dessert a unique praline flavor that takes the taste of pancakes and other desserts to a new level.
Yield: 4 servings
Total Time Taken: 15 minutes
Ingredients
8-ounce butter, divided
2 teaspoons soy sauce
2 teaspoons vanilla extract
2 teaspoons honey
Directions

1. Place a small saucepan over medium heat, add 2-ounce butter and let heat until completely melted and browned, don't' burn the butter.
2. Stir in soy sauce and then transfer into a bowl. Using a hand blender, gradually blend in remaining butter until smooth and fluffy. Then whisk in vanilla and honey and serve.
   Nutritional Information Per Serving: 171 Cal, 15 g total fat (5 g sat. fat), 40 mg chol., 100 mg sodium, 7 g carb., 0 g fiber, 1 g protein.

19. Chocolate & Peanut Squares

Chocoholics will love this chocolaty goodness. Chocolate and peanut butter combination is just wow!
Yield: 12 servings
Total Time Taken: 40 minutes
Ingredients
3½ ounce dark chocolate
4 tablespoons butter
1/8 teaspoon salt
3 ⅓ tablespoons peanut butter
½ teaspoon vanilla extract
1 teaspoon ground cinnamon
3⅓ tablespoons chopped salted peanuts
Directions

1. In a microwave ovenproof bowl place chocolate and butter and microwave at high heat setting for 1 minute or until completely melted, stir halfway.
2. Into the melted chocolate whisk in remaining ingredients until combined and then pour the mixture into a small baking dish, greased with oil.
3. Let mixture stand at room temperature for 20 minutes or until slightly cool and then scatter peanut across the top.
4. Place dish in the refrigerator or until set and slightly firm. Cut into squares to serve.
   Nutritional Information Per Serving: 317 Cal, 21 g total fat (11 g sat. fat), 143 mg chol., 392 mg sodium, 21 g carb., 1G fiber, 11 g protein.

TRIFLE

This cake layered creamy pudding dessert will give you freshness and delicious combination of avocado and coconut. It is not only gorgeous and delicious, but also easy to prepare.

Yield: 4 servings

Total Time Taken: 20 minutes

Ingredients

1 small banana, peeled and chopped

1 medium-sized avocado, peeled and pitted

6-ounce coconut cream

1 tablespoon lime juice

1/8 teaspoon lime zest

1 tablespoon vanilla extract

3 ½ ounce raspberries, fresh

2 ounce roasted pecan nuts

Directions

1. In a bowl place ½ tablespoon of vanilla and add banana and coconut cream. Chop avocado, add to banana mixture and stir until combined.
2. In another bowl, place remaining vanilla and add berries. Stir until mixed well.
3. Fill the dessert glasses with prepared banana-avocado mixture and berries mixture in alternate layers and then top with nuts. Serve straightaway.

Nutritional Information Per Serving: 317 Cal, 21 g total fat (11 g sat. fat), 143 mg chol., 392 mg sodium, 21 g carb., 1G fiber, 11 g protein.

20.   Chocolate Mouse

A simple to make and tempting chocolate mousse that you can whip up within 10 minutes. Freeze it to get a low-carb ice cream.

Yield: 6 servings

Total Time Taken: 10 minutes

Ingredients

3 1/3 cups coconut milk, chilled

3 tablespoons cocoa powder, unsweetened

1 teaspoon vanilla extract

1 teaspoon honey

Directions

1. Separate cream from coconut milk and place in a bowl. Add vanilla and honey and whisk using a hand blender until the mixture reaches desired thickness.
2. Then whisk in cocoa powder and spoon mousse into the serving bowl to serve.

Nutritional Information Per Serving: 317 Cal, 21 g total fat (11 g sat. fat), 143 mg chol., 392 mg sodium, 21 g carb., 1G fiber, 11 g protein.

21.Low Carb Choco Chip Brownie

This low carb brownie with extra chocolate chips tastes amazing.

Makes: 16 servings

Prep: 30 min

Bake: 15 min at 350°F

Ingredients:

¾ cup blanched almond flour

1 tsp baking powder

2 tbsps. Organic cocoa powder

¼ tsp salt

2 tbsps. Dark chocolate chips

2 tbsps. White chocolate chips

1 cup sweetener
3 eggs
½ tsp vanilla extract
8 tbsps. Butter, softened
Directions:-
1. Preheat oven at 350°F. Grease 9 inch baking pan
2. Combine the first four ingredients in a bowl and mix well
3. Except chocolate chips blend the remaining wet ingredients until smooth. Slowly add dry ingredients and fold to mix. Add chocolate chips and fold.
4. Pour the mixture in pan and bake for 30 minutes
Nutritional Value per serving: 122 Cal, 12.31 g total fat, 3.11 g protein, 3.1 g carb.

22.   Buffalo Wings

This combination of chicken and buffalo sauce is a win-win and creates an ultimate hot wing. Its texture and taste is exactly like the classic hot wings served at restaurants.
Yield: 3 servings
Total Time Taken: 20 minutes
Ingredients
12 chicken wings
4 tablespoons butter, unsalted
¼ cup hot sauce
1 teaspoon minced garlic
¼ teaspoon paprika
¼ teaspoon cayenne pepper
1 ¼ tablespoon salt
½ teaspoon ground black pepper
2 tablespoons olive oil
Directions
1. Set oven to 450 degrees F and let preheat.
2. In the meantime, rinse chicken wings, pat dry and place in a large bowl. Add oil, 1 tablespoon salt, ¼ teaspoon black pepper and toss to coat. Then arrange chicken wings in two large rimmed baking sheets in a single layer.
3. Place baking sheets into the oven and bake for 20-25 minutes or until meat is no longer pink and is tender.
4. In the meantime, prepare buffalo sauce. Place butter and garlic in a microwave ovenproof bowl and microwave for 1 minute or until butter melts completely, stir halfway.
5. When the butter is melted stir in remaining ingredients until smooth.
6. Transfer baked chicken wings into a large bowl, add buffalo sauce and toss to coat. Serve immediately.
Nutritional Information Per Serving: 542 Cal, 35 g total fat (13.8 g sat. fat), 133 mg chol., 2043 mg sodium, 8 g carb., 3 g fiber, 46.8 g protein.

23.   Salted Almonds

A handful of crispy almonds makes a great go-to snack to hold hunger until dinner. This is a nice way to add nuts into the keto diet.
Yield: 2 servings
Total Time Taken: 20 minutes
Ingredients
1 pound almonds, raw
1 ¼ tablespoon salt and more as needed
Water as needed
Filtered water

Directions

1. In a bowl place almonds, sprinkle with salt and then fill with water enough to cover nuts by 3 inches. Let rest in a warm place for 4 hours or overnight.
2. Then strain almonds and return to the bowl. Season with salt to taste and serve.
Nutritional Information Per Serving: 170 Cal, 16 g total fat (1.5 g sat. fat), 0 mg chol., 200 mg sodium, 6 g carb., 3 g fiber, 6 g protein.

24. Thyme & Onion Crackers

Crunchy thyme and onion crackers are nut-free, grain-free and loaded with savory flavors. They are a perfect substitute for whole wheat crackers.

Yield: 75 servings
Total Time Taken: 2 hours and 10 minutes
Ingredients
1 large sweet onion, peeled and chopped
1 teaspoon minced garlic
2 teaspoons thyme leaves, fresh
½ teaspoon salt
½ teaspoon ground black pepper
¼ cup olive oil
1½ cups flax seeds, grounded
¼ cup sunflower seeds, grounded
Directions

1. Set oven to 225 degrees F temperature and let preheat.
2. In a food processor place onion, add garlic, thyme, salt, pepper and oil and pulse until smooth. Then add flax seeds and sunflower seeds and blend until combined.
3. Tip the mixture into a bowl and shape ½ cup of this mixture into a ball.
4. Cut out 10 inches wide piece from parchment paper and then place the prepared ball in the middle, one side of the parchment. Fold the other side of parchment over the ball, like a book, and roll using a rolling pin until mixture is ¼ inch thick.
5. Fold away and cut off the top halfway of parchment, then using a sharp knife cut cracker mixture into 1-inch cube. Remove excess cracker mixture and arrange cracker cubes with the parchment on a baking sheet.
6. Repeat this procedure for the remaining cracker mixture, cut out cubes and then place on another baking sheet.
7. Place baking sheets filled with cracker cubes for 2 hours or until crispy and dry, switch position of sheets halfway through and remove the bottom parchment sheet.
8. Let cracker cool on wire rack for 15 minutes before serving.
Nutritional Information Per Serving: 130 Cal, 8 g total fat (0 g sat. fat), 0 mg chol., 0 mg sodium, 4.5 g carb., 3 g fiber, 6 g protein.

25. Nut Hummus

This is a quick and easy nut-based hummus keto recipe. It comes out within 5 minutes and feels so good in every way possible.

Yield: 8 servings
Total Time Taken: 3 minutes
Ingredients
1 cup macadamia nuts, soaked
3 garlic cloves
2 tablespoons tahini paste
½ teaspoon salt
½ teaspoon ground pepper
1/8 teaspoon cayenne pepper

3 tablespoons lemon juice
3 tablespoons water
Directions
1. In a food processor or blender place all the ingredients and pulse until smooth.
2. Tip hummus into serving bowl and serve with crackers, chips or vegetable wedges.
   Nutritional Information Per Serving: 80 Cal, 7 g total fat (1 g sat. fat), 0 mg chol., 130 mg sodium, 4.3 g carb., 1 g fiber, 2 g protein.

26. Sweet Chicken Wrapped in Bacon

In this recipe, bacon wrapped chicken bites are presented with a twist in their classic flavor. They are tender, juicy and an easy one-bite snack, side, and appetizer.
Yield: 15 servings
Total Time Taken: 55 minutes
Ingredients
1 ¼ pounds chicken breasts
1 pound slices of bacon, raw
2 tablespoons red chili powder
2/3 cup brown sugar, packed
Directions
1. Set oven to 350 degrees F and let preheat.
2. Take a large baking sheet, grease with oil and set aside until required.
3. Rinse chicken, pat dry and cut into 1-inch cubes.
4. In a small bowl mix together red chili powder and sugar until combined.
5. Cut each slice of bacon into thirds and then wrap each chicken piece with a bacon slice. Secure with a toothpick, then dredge into prepared spice mix to coat and place on the prepared baking sheet.
6. Place the baking sheet into the oven and bake bites for 30-35 minutes or until meat is cooked through. Then turn on broiler and cook for 2-3 minutes or until bacon is crispy. Serve warm.
   Nutritional Information Per Serving: 390 Cal, 22.5 g total fat (4.7 g sat. fat), 46 mg chol., 877 mg sodium, 12 g carb., 1.6 g fiber, 19 g protein.

27. Summer Salad

Crunchy salads are a perfect and refreshing snack on a hot summer day. Make your own version of low-carb summer salad by adding or cutting the ingredients.
Yield: 4 servings
Total Time Taken: 10 minutes
Ingredients
1 medium-sized red onion, peeled and chopped
2 large tomatoes, cubed
1 medium-sized green bell peppers, seeded and cubed
1 medium-sized cucumber, stemmed and cubed
1 medium-sized avocado, peeled and pitted
1 medium carrot, peeled and shredded
2 lemons, juiced
2 tablespoons Italian seasoning
Directions
1. Prepare all the vegetables and place in a bowl. Then drizzle with lemon juice and sprinkle with Italian seasoning.
2. Toss until mixed and serve straightaway.
   Nutritional Information Per Serving: 38.8 Cal, 1.4 g total fat (0.1 g sat. fat), 0.2 mg chol., 144 mg sodium, 0.2 g carb., 2.8 g fiber, 2.3 g protein.

VEGETARIAN KETO DESSERTS

28.   Turnip Fries

A healthy replacement for unhealthy French fries.
Makes: 6 servings
Prep: 10 min
Cook: 15 min
Ingredients:
Organic turnips (peeled, chopped as finger chips) – 2 lbs.
Sea salt (unrefined) – ½ teaspoon
Taco seasoning – 2 tablespoon
Organic light olive oil – ¼ cup
Directions:-

1. Combine all the ingredients in a Ziploc bag and shake well to mix.
2. Spread on a baking sheet lined with parchment paper.
3. Bake in an oven preheated to 350 degrees Fahrenheit for 25 minutes until golden brown, tossing in between.
   Nutritional Value per serving: 129 Cal, 9.5 g total fat (1.3 g sat. fat), 7.7 g net carbs, 3.3 g fiber, 1.7 g protein.

29.   Chocolate Mousse

Try these chocolate fat bombs and they help you overcome cravings for sugar.
Makes: 4 servings
Prep Time: 5 min
Ingredients
1 cup of creamed coconut milk
3 tbsps. of raw cocoa powder
½ tsp of cinnamon
6-12 drops of liquid stevia extract
Shredded coconut for garnish
Directions

1. Put a coconut milk can into your fridge overnight. Once thick, put it into a bowl.
2. Whip in raw cocoa powder.
3. Add in cinnamon and stevia.
4. Whip until it's smooth and creamy.
5. Place in serving glass then garnish using some pinch of shredded coconut. Enjoy!
   Nutritional information per serving: Total carbs 13.5g, Fiber 5.8g, Protein 6.2g, Fat 42.9G, Magnesium 75mg, Potassium 520MG

30.   Cream Cheese and Peanut Butter Fat Bomb

Try this creamy and deliciously sweet fat bomb for your family.
Makes: 14 pieces
Prep Time: 10 min
Ingredients
1 cup of heavy whipping cream
3 Tablespoons of BP2 peanut butter, powdered
2 Tablespoons of Splenda
2 Tablespoons of sour cream
4 Tablespoons of softened cream cheese
Directions

1. Whip heavy whipping cream for it to be light and airy. Add the remaining ingredients and mix well.

2. Spoon into some silicone candy mold tray to make 14 portions then freeze overnight.
3. Serve them partially frozen or allow to defrost completely for fluffy treat.
   Nutritional information per serving: Calories 82, Total fat 8g, Cholesterol 24MG, Sodium 29MG, Totals carbs 1G, Protein 1G

31. Ginger Fat Bombs

These fat bombs will provide you with an easy-to-make snack.
Makes: 10 servings
Prep Time: 10 min
Ingredients
75g / 2.6OZ of coconut butter
75g / 2.6OZ of coconut oil
25G / 1OZ of shredded/desiccated coconut
1 tsp of granulated sweetener
1/2-1 tsp of ginger powder
Directions
1. Mix all your ingredients in some pouring jug until your sweetener becomes dissolved.
2. Pour into some silicon molds or some ice block trays then refrigerate for around 10 minutes.
   Nutritional information per serving: Calories 120, Total Fat 12.8G, Fiber 1.4g, Sugars 0.1G, Protein 0.5g

32. Chocolate Fat Bombs

Try these simple fat bombs and enjoy the delicacy of chocolate.
Makes: 14 servings
Prep Time: 10 min
Ingredients
125g / 4.5OZ of coconut oil
25G / 1OZ of unsweetened cocoa powder
1 tbsp. of granulated sweetener
1-2 tbsps. Of tahini paste
25G / 1OZ of walnut halves
Directions
1. Warm your coconut oil until becomes melted.
2. Add the other ingredients (other than walnuts) then allow to cool so that ingredients do not settle and sink to bottom of your fat bomb.
3. Pour into the ice cube trays then refrigerate until it is semi set.
4. Once it's almost set, put half walnut on the top of every fat bomb.
   Nutritional information per serving: Calories 119, Total fat 12.6G, Total carbs 1.2G, Protein 1.4G

33. Orange Pecan Butter Fat Bombs

Make these fat bombs and enjoy the delicacy of butter in it.
Makes: 2 servings
Prep Time: 10 min
Ingredients
4 toasted pecan halves
1/2 tbsp. of unsalted grass-fed butter
1/2 tsp of orange zest, finely grated
1 pinch of sea salt
Directions
1. Toast your pecans at 350° in an oven for about 8-10 minutes, then keep aside to cool.
2. Soften butter, then add orange zest then mix well until it becomes smooth and creamy.
3. Spread half of butter-orange mixture in two pecan halves. Sprinkle using sea salt then enjoy.

Nutritional information per serving: Calories 89, Net carbs 1

34. Mocha Vanilla Fat Bomb Pops

Make these fat bombs and enjoy them when frozen.

Makes: 6 servings

Prep Time: 10 min

Ingredients

4 tbsps. of unsalted butter

2 tbsps. of heavy cream

1/2 tsp of vanilla extract

4 tbsps. of coconut oil

1/2 tbsp. of unsweetened cocoa powder

1/2 tsp of coffee extract

Stevia, to taste

Directions

1. **Make vanilla layer:**
2. Soften butter in a microwave until liquefied.
3. Add the heavy cream then stir. Keep aside.
4. Once cooled, add in vanilla then blend well.
5. Pour vanilla mixture into the muffin liners/tins. Place into your refrigerator until it is firm.
   Make mocha layer:
1. Mix coconut oil, coffee extract, cocoa powder and stevia.
2. Remove the vanilla layer from fridge then pour in mocha mixture, while filling the cups to top.
3. Add the popsicle sticks then freeze for 20 to 30 minutes.
   Nutritional Value per serving: 167 Calories; trace Protein, 19g Fat, .5g Dietary Fiber, 1G Carbohydrate

35. Mocha Ice Bombs

Make these frozen fat bombs and they will help you overcome hunger.

Makes: 12 servings

Prep Time: 10 min

Ingredients

Mocha Ice Bombs

1CUP of cream cheese 1/4CUPOF powdered sweetener 2 tbsp. of unsweetened cocoa 1/4CUP of strong coffee chilled

Chocolate coating

70g of melted chocolate

28G of melted cocoa butter

Directions

1. Add coffee to cream cheese, the cocoa, and the sweetener.
2. Blend until smooth.
3. To make ice bomb shape, just roll 2 tablespoons of mocha ice bomb mixture then place them on a tray or a plate lined with a baking parchment.
   Chocolate coating
1. Mix your melted chocolate and the cocoa butter together.
2. Roll every ice bomb in chocolate coating then place back on a lined tray/plate.
3. Place in a freezer for about 2 hours.
   Nutritional information per serving: Calories 127, Total fat 12.9G, Total carbs 2.2G, Protein 1.9G

36. Roasted Radish Chips

Snack on these chips while watching a movie.
Makes: 4 servings
Prep: 10 min
Cook: 15 min
Ingredients:
Fresh radish (chopped thinly into rounds) – 16 oz.
Sea salt – ½ teaspoon
Pepper – ½ teaspoon
Coconut oil – 2 tablespoon
Directions:-
1. Toss together all the ingredients and spread on baking sheets with any overlap.
2. Bake in an oven preheated to 400 degrees Fahrenheit for another 12-15 minutes.
   Nutritional Value per serving: 70 Cal, 7.1 g total fat (6 g sat. fat), 0 mg chol., 304 mg sodium, 2.2 g carbs, 1 g fiber, 0.4 g protein.

37.   Lime Avocado Popsicle
On a hot summer day, this popsicle is something you will yearn for.
Makes: 6 servings
Prep: 5 min
Cook: 3 min
Ingredients:
Avocados - 2
Coconut milk – 1 ½ cup
Erythritol – ¼ cup
Lime juice – 2 tablespoon
Directions:-
1. Blend all the ingredients together in a blender until creamy and smooth.
2. Distribute the blended mixture into 6 Popsicle molds and tap to remove an air bubbles.
3. Place Popsicle sticks into the mold centers and freeze for 7-8 hours.
4. Before removing the popsicles, run water on the mold.
   Nutritional Value per serving: 220 Cal, 21.9 g total fat (12.1 sat. fat), 0 mg chol., 12.1 mg sodium, 7.7 g carbs, 4.5 g fiber, 2.5 g protein.

38.   Raspberry Chia Pudding
A great dessert to prepare for a party.
Makes: 4 servings
Prep: 5 min
Ingredients:
Coconut milk – 1 cup
Water – ½ cup
Fresh raspberries – 1 cup
Whole chia seeds – ½ cup
Vanilla powder – 1 teaspoon
Directions:-
1. Combine the water, raspberries and coconut milk in a blender and pulse until smooth.
2. Mix together the blended mixture, chia seeds and vanilla.
3. Refrigerate overnight.
   Nutritional Value per serving: 223 Cal, 18.2 g total fat (11.3 g sat. fat), 12 g carbs, 7.7 g fiber, 5.5 g protein.

39.   Zucchini Chips
Make a double dose of these, because they are going to be finished in no time.

Makes: 8 servings
Prep: 15 min
Cook: 2-3 hours
Ingredients:
Zucchini (sliced thinly) – 4 cups
White balsamic vinegar – 2 tablespoons
Extra-virgin olive oil – 2 tablespoon
Coarse sea salt – 2 teaspoons
Directions:-
1. Whisk together the vinegar and oil in a bowl and toss the zucchini in it.
2. Place the zucchini in a cookie sheet lined with parchment paper in an even layer and sprinkle salt on them.
3. Bake for 2-3 hours at 200 degrees Fahrenheit, flipping halfway during the cook time.
Nutritional Value per serving: 40 Cal, 3.6 g total fat (0.5 sat. fat), 0 mg chol., 571 mg sodium, 2.9 g carbs, 0.6 g fiber, 0.7 g protein.

40.   Raspberry Coconut Bark

This makes a yummy fat bomb recipe.
Makes: 12 servings
Prep: 10 min
Cook: minutes
Ingredients:
Dried raspberries (frozen) – ½ cup
Coconut butter – ½ cup
Coconut oil – ½ cup
Shredded coconut (unsweetened) – ½ cup
Swerve sweetener (powdered) – ¼ cup
Directions:-
1. Powder the frozen berries in a food processor. Leave aside.
2. Combine the rest of the ingredients in a saucepan over low flame, stirring frequently until melted.
3. Pour half the pan mixture into a baking pan lined with parchment paper.
4. Mix the powdered berries into the remaining pan mixture, stirring well.
5. Spoon the raspberry mixture over the coconut mix in the baking pan and swirl it using a knife.
6. Freeze until you can break into pieces.
Nutritional Value per serving: 234 Cal, 23.56 g total fat (10.3 g sat. fat), 6.56 g carbs, 4.11 g fiber, 1.72 g protein.

41. Choco-Peppermint Fudge

Make this for your kid's birthday party.
Makes: 24 servings
Prep: 5 min
Cook: 5 minutes
Ingredients:
Cacao butter – 4 oz.
Coconut milk – 1 can
Coconut oil – ½ cup
Soft coconut butter – 1 cup
Swerve sweetener – ½ cup
Vanilla protein powder – ½ cup
Peppermint extract – 1 teaspoon

Peppermint stevia – 1 teaspoon
Salt – ¼ teaspoon
Crushed candy canes (sugar-free) – for topping
Directions:-

1. Place the cacao butter in a saucepan over low flame until it melts and then mix in the coconut butter, coconut milk and coconut oil, stirring continuously until smooth.
2. Remove from the flame and whisk in the vanilla protein powder, peppermint extract, salt, stevia and sweetener.
3. Transfer the mixture into a pan lined with parchment paper and sprinkle crushed candy canes on it.
4. Refrigerate overnight and then chop.
   Nutritional Value per serving: 129 Cal, 13.6 g total fat (10.3 g sat. fat), 2 mg chol., 41 mg sodium, 2.1 g carbs, 1.1 g fiber, 1.3 g protein.

42.   Strawberry Mousse Pie

A delectable dessert pie everyone will love, this highly versatile strawberry mousse pie can be made with blueberries, cranberries or raspberries too.
Serves 12
15 minutes
Ingredients:
1 Healthy Pie Crust
½ cup fresh Strawberries
1 cup Cream Cheese, softened
2 tablespoons Water
½ tablespoon Lemon Juice
½ cup Heavy Cream
1 teaspoon Gelatin
¼ teaspoon Berry-flavored Stevia Drops
1 cup fresh Strawberries, cut into slices
For the Topping:
2 cups Heavy Cream
12 teaspoon Vanilla-flavored Stevia Drops
Directions:-

1. Prepare the pie crust by rolling out the pie crust dough and transferring to a pie plate. Place in the fridge to chill while you prepare the pie filling and topping.
2. Heat 2 tablespoons of water in a small pan and pour gelatin in. Let the mixture cook over low heat, stirring to dissolve the gelatin. Set aside to let cool.
3. Add the cream cheese, strawberries, lemon juice and berry-flavored stevia drops in a food processor and blend until creamy.
4. Transfer the mixture over to an electric mixer and pour in the heavy cream. Beat on high speed until mixture has been thoroughly whipped. Pour in the gelatin one tablespoon at a time and blend for about a minute.
5. Spoon the mixture into the prepared pie crust and spread evenly.
6. To serve, layer sliced strawberries on top.
7. Prepare the topping by mixing the heavy cream and vanilla drops until soft peaks form. Spoon the mixture over the sliced strawberries and spread evenly.
   Nutritional Value per serving: Total calories 382G, protein 5.5g, total fat 40.5g, total carbohydrates 5.5g, cholesterol 100MG, sodium 178mg

43.   Walnut Brownie

Surprise your guest with this tasty low carb walnut brownie making them come for more!
Makes: 4 servings

Prep: 45 min
Bake: 30 min at 350°F
Ingredients:
1/3 cup sweetener of your choice
6 tbsps. Butter
1/3 cup organic cocoa powder
½ tsp vanilla extract
1 egg
¼ cup almond flour
½ tsp salt
½ tsp baking powder
1/3 cup chopped walnuts
Directions:-
Preheat oven on 350°F. Grease 9 inch square baking tray
In a bowl add the first five ingredients and beat well to a smooth mixture
Slowly add flour along with the remaining ingredients and fold in gently
Pour the mixture in tray and bake for 30 minutes
Nutritional Value per serving: 290 Cal, 18.5 g total fat, 3.8 g protein, 3 g carb.

44.   Simple Taco Pie

The 2 best comfort foods come together in this savory meat and eggs pie that everyone in the family will love!
Serves 8
45 minutes
Ingredients:
1 pound ground Beef
2 cloves Garlic, finely chopped
1 cup Cheddar, grated
6 Eggs
1 cup Heavy Cream
¾ cup Water
3 tablespoons Taco Seasoning
½ teaspoon Salt
¼ teaspoon Pepper
Directions:-

1. Have the oven pre-heated to 350 degrees and lightly grease a pie plate, set aside.
2. Heat up 1 tablespoon of olive oil in a medium skillet and brown ground beef, cooking for about 7-8 minutes.
3. Pour the taco seasonings in and stir to combine well, after which pour the water in and reduce heat to medium-low and continue cooking until the mixture has thickened.
4. Transfer the beef mixture to the prepared pie plate.
5. Whisk together eggs, cream, garlic, salt and pepper in a large mixing bowl. Pour this mixture over the beef mixture already in the pie plate.
6. Top evenly with the grated cheddar cheese and bake for 30 minutes.
7. Garnish with diced avocados, sour cream, diced tomatoes and chopped cilantro to serve.
   Nutritional Value per serving: Total calories 302G, protein 20G, total fat 21G, total carbohydrates 2G, cholesterol 215MG, sodium 187mg

45.   Choco Burst Brownie

Treat your taste buds with extra dose of chocolate and bits of crispy nuts in every bite.
Makes: 25 servings
Prep: 60 min

Bake: 40 min at 350°F
Ingredients:
1 ½ cups soy flour
1 ½ tbsps. Oats bran
½ cup butter
4 ounce baking chocolate
2 cups sugar substitute
5 eggs
½ cup cream
2 tsp baking powder
1 teaspoon vanilla extract
½ cup chopped walnuts
For frosting
5 tbsps. Cocoa powder
1 cup sugar substitute
3 tbsps. Unsalted butter
1 tsp vanilla
1/3 cup cream
Directions:-
1. Preheat oven on 350°F. Grease 9 inch square baking pan
2. Melt butter with chocolate in a pan. Add sugar stir in to melt. Switch off heat and let the mixture cool
3. Beat in eggs with vanilla into the chocolate mixture until smooth
4. In a bowl mix baking powder, cream, flour and walnut. Slowly add the mixture into the chocolate batter and fold in. Pour the batter in pan and bake for 35-40 minutes.
5. For frosting blend all the frosting ingredients until smooth and spread on cooled brownies
Nutritional Value per serving: 152 Cal, 14 g total fat, 2 g protein, 6 g carb.

46.   White Chocolate Bars

One can never have too much chocolate, and depending on the molds you use, this can be a very special gift for someone.
Serves 6
Prep time: 15 minutes
Ingredients
2.5 oz cocoa butter
3 tbsps. Swerve
1 tbsp. coconut milk powder
1 tsp sunflower lecithin
1/8 tsp stevia extract powder
1/8 tsp monk fruit powder
1/2 tsp vanilla extract
Directions
1. Put a pan on a pot with boiling water and melt, in a pan, coconut milk powder, cocoa butter, swerve, stevia, lecithin, and monk fruit.
2. Remove the pan from the stove and start adding vanilla.
3. Pour the batter into the molds, and put them in the fridge. When their consistency is solid, you can remove them from the molds.
Nutritional Value per serving
Net carbs: 0.6g, Fat: 8.1G, Fiber: 0g, Protein: 0g, CALORIES:123G

47.   Creme Brulee

Crème Brulee – a burnt crème, a fantastically decadent and seductive dessert. Now, in a new, healthy disguise.

Serves 4

Prep time: 1 hour, 15 minutes

Ingredients

2 cups heavy cream

1 vanilla bean

⅓ Tsp stevia powder

4 egg yolks

1 tsp vanilla extract

Pinch salt

4 tbsps. erythritol for sprinkling

Directions

1. Put 2 cups of heavy cream into the pan and heat it on medium heat. After couple of minutes, add vanilla. (We recommend using vanilla bean seeds, because they give nice texture). When the cream starts to bubble, set it, covered, on low for 20 minutes, and chill it for couple of minutes.
2. In a mixing bowl, put yolks, vanilla extract, salt and stevia and beat them until the crème gets a pale color and thicker texture.
3. Continue whisking the eggs, and while doing so, very, very slowly start adding the heavy crème, thus bringing the eggs to a higher temperature. This batter should have a nice and pale color.
4. In a casserole or baking dish, put 4 baking, ceramic cups and pour the batter in. Pour the water in the dish (half of the cup's height).Put the casserole on the middle rack in the oven and bake for 30-35 minutes at 300F. They should have a texture like jelly, and should sit in the fridge overnight.
5. Before serving, put small amount (1 tablespoon) of erythritol or stevia on top of each brulee, put them on a baking tray and place them on a highest rack in the oven.
6. When they get golden color they are done, but be careful because they caramelize quickly.

Nutritional Value per serving

Net carbs: 3.8g, Fat: 44.5g, Protein: 2.7G, Calories: 450

48.　　Mint Chocolate Chip Ice-Cream

This ice-cream has it all what is needed for summer – a refreshing mint flavor, combined with more satisfying taste of a chocolate.

Serves 8

Prep time: 1 hour

Ingredients

2 large avocados

2 cups coconut milk

½ cup powdered erythritol

15-20 drops stevia extract

1 tbsp. vanilla extract or 1 vanilla bean

¼ cup fresh mint or more to taste or just use mint extract

½ - 1 tbsp. mint extract

1 package dark chocolate chips

Directions

1. Cat the avocado on half and spoon it.
2. Put the avocado pulp, coconut milk, erythritol, stevia and mint and vanilla extract into the mixing bowl, and mix them until the batter is smooth and there are no lumps.
3. Freeze the coconut crème and blend it with avocado mixture. When the mixture is nicely combined, add dark chocolate chips, and use a spoon to mix it, so the chips are distributed evenly

4. Put it in a freezer and let it sit there for 30-60 minutes.
   Nutritional Value per serving
   Net carbs: 5.7, Fiber: 4.8g, Fat: 25.3g, Protein: 3.6g, Calories: 268

49.   Lemon Cheesecake Mousse

This is a very girly recipe, very refreshing, creamy and very pretty. Just the right thing for little girls!
Serves 5
Prep time: 10 minutes
Ingredients
8 oz. mascarpone cheese (or cream cheese, if you don't have it)
1/4 cup fresh lemon juice
1 cup heavy cream
1/2-1 tsp liquid stevia
1/8 tsp salt
Directions
1. Mix the lemon juice and cream cheese with mixer and blend until the batter is smooth.
2. When the mixture is ready, add a heavy whipping cream, stevia and salt.
3. If you want it to be sweeter, add more stevia.
4. Put the crème into the piping bag and pipe it in high serving glasses. Garnish with lemon zest and keep them in a fridge.
   Nutritional Value per serving
   Net carbs: 1.7G, Fat: 29.6g, Protein: 3.7g, Calories: 277

50.   Zabaglione Meringues

This is a keto twist of an old, Italian dessert, enjoyed by everybody with foamy cream and delicious and crunchy meringues.
Serves 6
Prep time: 3 hours, 45 minutes
Ingredients
6 medium eggs, divided
1 gram powdered stevia
3 strawberries
Zest of 1 lemon
1 stick butter
4 tbsps. coconut oil
2 tsp vanilla extract (divided)
1 cup heavy whipping cream
Directions
1. Separate the eggs and put in bowl egg whites, 1 tsp vanilla and ½ stevia. Start beating the egg whites and beat them until they are stiff. Put 1/3 of this batter in another bowl and put it on a side.
2. Put the batter into a pastry bag and spoon little round meringues in on a parchment paper.
3. Preheat your oven to 200 degrees and put the tray with egg whites in it. Leave the doors slightly open.
4. For Zabaglione you must melt the coconut oil and the butter, in a pan (make a double boiler).
5. Wash and trim strawberries, and put them, together with lemon zest and rest of stevia and vanilla in a blender.
6. In the meantime, start mixing the eggs until foamy and add strawberries in them, then, slowly and gently start pouring that mixture into the butter mixture. While doing so, keep mixing it on the slowest setting.

7. Add in the mixture the rest of the egg whites, and mix them in it very gently. Cook that mixture for 5 minutes and constantly mix it, so it does not stick.
8. When done, it should have a nice a light texture. Take it off the stove, and let it cool down.
9. Make the heavy whipping cream.
10. Serve it in nice, glass, serving bowl by adding little meringues and whipping cream on top. Store it in a fridge.
   Nutritional Value per serving
   Net carbs: 2.97G, Fat: 36g, Protein: 6.66g, Calories: 367

51. Nutty Chocolate
This is of those recipes that you can never have enough of. You will always come back for "just one more bite".
Serves 12
Prep time: 10 minutes
Ingredients
2.5 oz. tahini butter
2 oz. almond butter
2 tbsps. erythritol
Pinch of sea salt
½ tsp vanilla extract
4 oz. melted cacao butter
Directions
1. Put sesame (tahini) and almond butter in a blender together with vanilla, salt and erythritol and blend it on low for 10 sec, and then start adding melted cacao butter slowly. When you add the entire butter, blend it for 15 more seconds.
2. As soon as you finish blending, pour the mixture into silicone, chocolate mold. Cool it and put it in a fridge.
3. Store them in a fridge.
   Nutritional Value per serving
   Net carbs: 1.5G, Fat: 15g, Fiber: 1.1G, Protein: 2G, Calories: 146

52. Cream cheese Brownie Keto Cookies
These appetizing chewy brownie cookies are full of soft creamy cream cheese and rich chocolate. Low on carbs but with an ample amount of healthy fats, these are a must for people on the ketogenic diet.
Makes: 6 servings
Prep: 10 min
Cook/Bake: 8 min at 320°F
Ingredients: -
1 tbsp. cream cheese, chopped into small pieces
2 tbsp. ground flaxseed
1 tbsp. sweetener
1 egg, whisked
4 tbsp. almond flour
2 tbsp. unsweetened cocoa powder
Directions: -
1. Preheat oven to 320°F and prepare a baking sheet lined with parchment paper.
2. In a medium bowl, mix all the dry ingredients together well. Add in the whisked egg and beat until all the ingredients are combined.
3. Fold in the cream cheese.
4. Using a spoon, scoop cookie dough mixture and arrange on prepared baking sheet making sure to leave a gap between each cookie.

5. Bake in the preheated oven for 8 minutes or until fully cooked.
6. Allow to cool on the baking sheet completely before transferring the cookies on to a wire cooling rack to cool completely.
   Nutritional Value per serving: - 65 Cal, 4.3g Fat, 1.26G Carb., 3g Protein

53.　　Chocolate Chunk Keto Cookies

These easily made chocolate chunk keto cookies are nice and crisp on the outside but soft and chewy in the middle. Packed with chocolate chunks, these are great with a cold glass of milk.
Makes: 16 servings
Prep: 10 min
Cook/Bake: 12 min at 350°F
Ingredients: -
1 cup 95% chocolate bar, chopped
1/2 tsp. baking powder
1/4 cup erythritol
8 tbsp. unsalted butter, softened
2 tbsp. coconut flour
1 cup almond flour
1 large egg
10 drops liquid stevia
2 tsp. vanilla extract
2 tbsp. psyllium husk
3 tbsp. unflavored whey protein powder
Directions: -
1. Preheat oven to 350°F and prepare a baking sheet lined with parchment paper.
2. In a medium bowl, mix all the dry ingredients well.
3. In a large bowl, add butter, erythritol, stevia and beat together. Add the egg and vanilla extract and mix well until all ingredients are combined. Gradually sift in the dry ingredients mixture, and stir well.
4. Using your hands, roll 16 cookie dough balls and arrange on prepared baking sheet. Using a wet glass, flatten the cookies slightly.
5. Bake in the preheated oven for 12 - 15 minutes or until firm.
6. Allow to cool on the baking sheet for a few minutes before transferring the cookies on to a wire cooling rack to cool completely.
   Nutritional Value per serving: - 118 Cal, 10.8g Fat, 1.6G Carb., 2.8G Fiber, 2.6G Protein

54.　　Cinnamon Butter Keto Cookies

These cookies will smell absolutely amazing when you bake these at home, filling your kitchen with the well-known baked cinnamon roll aroma.
Makes: 15 servings
Prep: 10 min
Cook/Bake: 18 min at 300°F
Ingredients: -
1 tsp. ground cinnamon
1/2 cup salted butter, softened
2 cups almond flour
1 tsp vanilla extract
1/2 cup Stevia
1 egg
Directions: -
1. Preheat oven to 300°F and prepare a baking sheet lined with parchment paper.
2. In a large bowl, combine all the ingredients and mix well until fully incorporated.

3. Using your hands, roll the cookie dough into 15 balls and place onto prepared baking sheet. Using a fork, press down on the cookies,
4. Bake in the preheated oven for roughly 18 - 25 minutes or until slightly brown.
5. Allow to cool on the baking sheet completely before transferring the cookies on to a wire cooling rack.
Nutritional Value per serving: - 141 Cal, 14G Fat, 2G Carb., 1G Sugars, 2G Fiber, 3g Protein

55.   Soft Brownie Keto Cookies

Addictive, soft, chewy brownies in cookie form to satisfy your sweet tooth. These easy to make brownie cookies are topped with flaked seat salt giving you the perfect salty and sweet combination.
Makes: 24 servings
Prep: 15 min
Cook/Bake: 10 min at 350°F
Ingredients: -
¼ tsp. sea salt
2 tbsp. tapioca starch
¼ tsp. coffee mix
¼ cup coconut oil
½ tsp. baking soda
¼ cup cacao powder
1 tsp. vanilla extract
8. oz chocolate chips, divided in half
1 cup coconut sugar
2 eggs
Sea salt flakes for sprinkling
Directions: -
1. Preheat oven to 350°F and prepare baking sheets lined with parchment paper.
2. Using a hand mixer or a stand mixer, mix the sugar and eggs until the mixture is light and fluffy.
3. In a separate bowl, melt the coconut oil, vanilla extract and chocolate chips together over a double boiler. Allow to slightly cool, then add this mixture to the egg mixture. Continue to mix until well combined.
4. In another bowl, whisk the tapioca starch, baking soda, sea salt, cacao powder and coffee mix. Pour this mixture into the wet mixture and mix again until well incorporated. Fold in the remaining chocolate chips.
5. Using a spoon or a scoop, scoop the cookie dough into mounds and place onto prepared baking sheet making sure to leave a 3-inch gap between each cookie. Sprinkle the cookies with sea salt flakes.
6. Bake in the preheated oven for roughly 10 - 12 minutes.
7. Allow to cool on the baking sheet for 10 minutes before transferring the cookies on to a wire cooling rack.
Nutritional Value per serving: - 71 Cal, 5g Fat, 7.5g Carb., 5.6g Sugars, less than 1G Fiber, less than 1G Protein

56. Fruity Amoretti Keto Cookies

This recipe is a spin on the well-known Italian amoretto cookies. With the same almond flavor, these thumbprint cookies are taken up a notch with fruity jam and sprinkles of coconut flakes.
Makes: 16 servings
Prep: 10 min
Cook/Bake: 16 min at 350°F
Ingredients: -

1 tbsp. shredded coconut
1/2 tsp. almond extract
4 tbsp. coconut oil
1/2 cup erythritol
1/2 tsp ground cinnamon
2 tbsp. coconut flour
1 cup almond flour
2 tbsp. sugar free jam
1/2 tsp. vanilla extract
2 large eggs
1/2 tsp. salt
1/2 tsp. baking powder
Directions: -
1. Preheat oven to 350°F and prepare a baking sheet lined with parchment paper.
2. In a large bowl, combine all the ingredients except for the shredded coconut, mix well until fully incorporated.
3. Using a spoon, scoop and arrange the cookie dough into ball onto prepared baking sheet. Using your finger, make an indent in the center of each cookie.
4. Bake in the preheated oven for roughly 16 minutes or until slightly brown.
5. Allow to cool on the baking sheet for a few minutes then spoon the jam on to each indent of the cookies. Sprinkle with shredded coconut then transfer the cookies on to a wire cooling rack to cool completely.
Nutritional Value per serving: - 86 Cal, 7.9g Fat, 1.2G Carb., 2.4G Protein

57.   Keto Candied Bacon Chocolate Chip Cookies

These Keto cookies aren't the most traditional but they certainly are a match made in heaven. Salty and sweet bacon with a generous drizzling of chocolate sauce. These homemade wonders are a great addition to your keto diet staples.
Makes: 24 servings
Prep: 25 min
Cook/Bake: 20 min at 350°F
Ingredients: -
1/2 tsp. vanilla extract
2 tbsp. scotch
1/2 cup erythritol
1 1/2 cup almond flour
6 slices candied bacon
1 tsp. baking powder
1 large egg
1/2 cup butter, softened
2/3 cup chocolate chips
Directions: -
1. Preheat oven to 350°F and prepare a baking sheet lined with parchment paper.
2. In a large bowl, combine erythritol, baking powder and almond flour. Mix well.
3. In a separate bowl, cream the butter with a hand mixer and add the egg, scotch and vanilla extract. Continue to mix until well incorporated.
4. Gradually add in the dry ingredients mixture, mix until a dough starts to form. Fold in chocolate chips.
5. Chop 2 slices of candied bacon and add to cookie dough. Fold in well.
6. Cover cookie dough with plastic wrap and place in the freezer to chill for 30 minutes.
7. Using your hands, roll 24 cookie dough balls and arrange on prepared baking sheet making sure to leave a 1-inch gap in between each cookie. Flatten the cookie dough balls.
8. Bake in the preheated oven for 20 - 22 minutes.

9. Chop remaining candied bacon strips and place on top of cookies.
10. Allow to cool on the baking sheet completely before transferring the cookies on to a wire cooling rack to cool completely.
   Nutritional Value per serving: - 106 Cal, 10.1G Fat, 1.3G Carb., 2.4G Fiber, 2.5g Protein

58.   Keto Chili Chocolate Cookies

This recipe takes the popular Mexican chili chocolate combination and puts it in cookie form. These chocolate cookies are topped off with a bit of chili. Not too spicy, but it definitely gives a little kick.
Makes: 15 servings
Prep: 10 min
Cook/Bake: 12 min at 350°F
Ingredients: -
1/2 tsp cayenne pepper
1 1/2 tsp chili powder
8 tbsp. unsweetened cocoa powder
2 tsp. vanilla
3 tbsp. salted butter, softened
3/4 cup coconut flour
2 1/2 tsp. ground cinnamon
1/2 cup sweetener
1/2 tsp. salt
4 large eggs
1/2 cup coconut oil
Directions: -
1. Preheat oven to 350°F and prepare a baking sheet lined with parchment paper.
2. In a large bowl, combine cocoa powder, cayenne pepper, sweetener, chili powder and salt. Mix well.
3. In a medium bowl, place butter a coconut oil. Mix well. Add eggs and vanilla extract and stir until well combined.
4. Add wet ingredients mixture to dry ingredients and mix well for a few minutes until all ingredients are incorporated.
5. Using your hands, roll 15 cookie dough balls and arrange on prepared baking sheet. Flatten the cookie dough balls.
6. Bake in the preheated oven for 12 - 15 minutes.
7. Allow to cool on the baking sheet completely before transferring the cookies on to a wire cooling rack to cool completely.
   Nutritional Value per serving: - 135 Cal, 12.3g Fat, 2.6G Carb., 2.5G Fiber, 2.9G Protein

59.   Keto Crunchy Peanut Butter Cookies

Everybody loves a peanut butter cookie and this recipe gives you that but in accordance to the Ketogenic diet. Low in carbs and high in healthy fats, these wonderful peanut butter cookies are delicious.
Makes: 20 servings
Prep: 10 min
Cook/Bake: 12 min at 320°F
Ingredients: -
1 tsp vanilla extract
1/2 cup xylitol
1 1/2 cup crunchy peanut butter
2 eggs
1/2 cup unsweetened shredded coconut

Directions: -
1. Preheat oven to 320°F and prepare a baking sheet lined with parchment paper.
2. In a large bowl, combine all the ingredients and mix well until fully incorporated.
3. Using your hands, roll the cookie dough into 20 balls and place onto prepared baking sheet. Flatten the cookie dough balls with your fingers.
4. Bake in the preheated oven for roughly 12 minutes or until slightly brown.
5. Allow to cool on the baking sheet completely before transferring the cookies on to a wire cooling rack.
Nutritional Value per serving: - 153 Cal, 11G Fat, 3g Carb., 1G Sugars, 2G Fiber, 4g Protein

60. Low Carb High Fat Pecan Coconut Flake Cookies

In thirty minutes, these scrumptious Pecan coconut cookies are baked in no time. Soft and chewy with crushed pecans and coconut flakes.
Makes: 12 servings
Prep: 10 min
Cook/Bake: 20 min at 350°F
Ingredients: -
1/4 tsp cinnamon
1/2 cup erythritol
2 tbsp. coconut oil
1/2 cup pecans, crushed
1/2 cup coconut flakes
1/2 cup peanut butter
1/2 tsp vanilla extract
2 large eggs
1/2 cup coconut flour
1/2 cup almond flour
Directions: -
1. Preheat oven to 350°F and prepare a baking sheet lined with parchment paper.
2. In a large bowl, combine all the ingredients and mix well until fully incorporated.
3. Using a spoon, scoop the cookie dough into 12 balls and arrange onto prepared baking sheet.
4. Bake in the preheated oven for roughly 20 minutes or until slightly brown.
5. Allow to cool on the baking sheet completely before transferring the cookies on to a wire cooling rack.
Nutritional Value per serving: - 171 Cal, 14G Fat, 4g Carb., 2G Sugars, 3g Fiber, 5g Protein

61.Low Carb High Fat Choco Coconut Cookies

These coconut macaroons are given a twist with the addition of rich cocoa powder. Chocolate goodness with coconut flavor, this simple to follow recipe only takes thirty minutes to whip up.
Makes: 20 servings
Prep: 10 min
Cook/Bake: 20 min at 350°F
Ingredients: -
1 tsp. vanilla extract
2 large eggs
½ cup unsweetened shredded coconut, extra for sprinkling
12 tsp. baking powder
3 tbsp. coconut flour
¼ cup coconut oil
¼ tsp. salt
1/3 cup erythritol
¼ cup cocoa powder

1 cup almond flour

Directions: -

1. Preheat oven to 350°F and prepare a baking sheet lined with parchment paper.
2. In a large bowl, combine the baking powder, cocoa powder, coconut flour, shredded coconut, almond flour and erythritol. Mix together well. Add the coconut oil, vanilla extract and eggs then stir well so that all the ingredients are incorporated.
3. Knead the cookie dough with your hands into a ball.
4. Using your hands, roll the cookie dough into small balls and arrange onto prepared baking sheet leaving a space between each cookie.
5. Bake in the preheated oven for roughly 15 - 20 minutes.
6. Sprinkle the extra shredded coconut on top of each cookie.
7. Allow to cool on the baking sheet completely before transferring the cookies on to a wire cooling rack.

Nutritional Value per serving: - 77 Cal, 7g Fat, 2.5G Carb., 1.5G Fiber, 2.2G Protein

62.   Low Carb High Fat Walnut Cookies

These soft and chewy walnut cookies are full of flavor, made with chopped walnuts and almond flour, these go wonderful with a hot cup of brewed coffee.

Makes: 18 servings
Prep: 5 min
Cook/Bake: 13 min at 350°F
Ingredients: -
1/2 tsp. baking soda
2 tbsp. erythritol
1 large egg
1/2 cup walnuts, chopped
1 1/2 cup almond flour
4 tbsp. butter, softened
Directions: -

1. Preheat oven to 350°F and prepare a baking sheet lined with parchment paper.
2. In a large bowl, combine all the ingredients and mix well until fully incorporated.
3. Using a spoon, scoop the cookie dough into 18 balls and arrange onto prepared baking sheet.
4. Bake in the preheated oven for roughly 13 minutes or until slightly brown.
5. Allow to cool on the baking sheet completely before transferring the cookies on to a wire cooling rack.

Nutritional Value per serving: - 101 Cal, 10G Fat, 1G Carb., 1G Sugars, 1G Fiber, 3g Protein

SWEET FAT BOMB RECIPES

63.   Blackberry Coconut Fat Bombs

Try these sugar-free low-carb fat bombs. Everyone in your family will enjoy them.

Makes: 6 servings
Prep Time: 5 minutes
Cook Time: 5 minutes
Total Time: 10 minutes
Ingredients
1 cup of coconut butter
1 cup of coconut oil
1/2 cup of frozen blackberries can
1/2 teaspoon of Sweat leaf Stevia drops
1/4 teaspoon of vanilla powder or a 1/2 teaspoon of vanilla extract
1 tablespoon of lemon juice
Directions

1. Place the coconut oil, coconut butter and blackberries in a pot then heat over a medium heat until they are well combined.
2. In some food processor or a small blender, add the berry mix and the remaining ingredients. Begin to process until they are smooth.
3. Spread out into some small pan readily lined with a parchment paper
4. Refrigerate for one hour.
5. Remove from the container then cut into squares.
6. Store while covered in a refrigerator.
   Nutritional information per serving: Calories 170 Calories from Fat 168, Total Fat 18.7g, Total carbohydrates 3g, Dietary Fiber 2.3g, Protein 1.1G

64.   Happy Almond Bombs

Make these fat bombs with a string coconut flavor.
Makes: 4 servings
Prep Time: 5 minutes
Cook Time: 5 minutes
Ingredients
4 tablespoons of almond butter
1OZ of cream cheese
4 tablespoons of coconut butter
1 tablespoons of cocoa powder
2 tablespoons of sugar free syrup
16G of dark chocolate
Directions

1. Add all the ingredientsother than coconut butter in some microwave-safe dish.
2. Microwave in intervals of 15 seconds, stirring frequently, until chocolate and the cream cheese have melted and all the ingredients have incorporated fully.
3. Add coconut butter, then mix all together fully.
4. Spoon the batter into 12 portions in a mini-muffin tray.
5. Pop these into a freezer for about 1 hour and they will be setup. Enjoy.
   Nutritional information per serving: calories 86, Total fat 7g, Total carbs 3g, protein 2G, cholesterol 3mg, sodium 21MG

65.   Strawberry Rhubarb Swirl Ice Cream Serves 6

Ingredients:
Strawberry Rhubarb Sauce:
1/2 teaspoon of Xanthan Gum
2 tablespoons of Granulated Stevia/Erythritol Blend
1 tablespoon of Water
1 teaspoon of Lemon Juice
1/2 cup of Diced Rhubarb
1/2 cup of Sliced Strawberries
Ice Cream:
16 ounces of Heavy Whipping Cream
1/2 cup of Granulated Stevia/Erythritol Blend
1/2 tablespoon of Vanilla Extract
3/4 cup of Unsweetened Almond Milk
Directions:
Strawberry Rhubarb Sauce:
1. In your medium-sized saucepan, combine your sweetener and xanthan gum.
2. Gradually whisk in water and lemon juice until combined.

3. Add your strawberries and rhubarb and bring saucepan to a medium heat, stirring frequently.

4. Heat your mixture until the rhubarb softens (approximately 4 to 6 minutes) and then remove from the heat. Allow the sauce to cool to room temperature before adding to the ice cream.

Ice Cream:

5. In your large-sized bowl, combine your heavy whipping cream, vanilla, and sweetener.

6. Using an electric mixer, whip your mixture until stiff peaks form.

7. Gradually add your almond milk, blending between each addition. Beat mixture until it re-thickens slightly.

8. Transfer your mixture to ice cream machine and freeze per manufacturer's instructions.

9. Once your mixture has reached the creamy texture of ice cream, transfer it to a freezer-safe container. Add the strawberry rhubarb sauce and swirl together with a spoon. Cool in freezer for approximately 2 to 3 hours before serving, stirring in 30-minute increments.

Nutritional Value per serving:

Calories: 285

Net Carbs: 3.6 grams

Fat: 29 grams

66. Strawberry Swirl Ice Cream Serves 6

Ingredients:

3 Large Egg Yolks

1 cup of Pureed Strawberries

1 cup of Heavy Cream

1/2 teaspoon of Vanilla Extract

1/3 cup of Erythritol

1 tablespoon of Vodka (Optional)

1/8 teaspoon of Xanthan Gum (Optional)

Directions:

1. Set a pot with your heavy cream over a low flame to heat up. Add in your erythritol.

2. Don't let your cream boil, just let it gently simmer till the erythritol is all dissolved.

3. Separate your egg yolks into a large mixing bowl. Beat with your electric mixer until doubled in size.

4. Temper your eggs so they don't scramble, add a couple tablespoons of the heated cream mixture at a time to the eggs while you're beating them.

5. Continue until your egg mixture is warm and then add in the rest of your cream mixture slowly, beating them constantly.

6. Add your vanilla extract and mix.

7. Optional step. Add your vodka and xanthan gum.

8. Place bowl in freezer and leave for 2 hours occasionally taking out to stir, Can also churn using your ice cream maker if you have one.

9. Puree your strawberries.

10. Once the ice cream has been chilled and is beginning to thicken add in your pureed strawberries.

11. Mix in your strawberries but don't mix too much. You want ribbons of your strawberry visible in the ice cream.

12. Place in freezer for 4 to 6 hours.

Nutritional Value per serving:

Calories: 178

Protein: 2 grams

Fat: 17 grams

Carbs: 3 grams

67.   Sugar-Free Lemon Curd

Ingredients:

2 Large Eggs

1/2 cup of Meyer Lemon Juice

2 Large Egg Yolks

2 tablespoons + 2 teaspoons of Truvia

6 tablespoons of Butter (Cut Into Cubes)

Directions:

1. Whisk your lemon juice, sweetener, eggs, and egg yolks together in your saucepan.

2. Add your butter and turn the heat up to a low temperature stirring continuously.

3. Once all of your butter has melted, turn the heat up to a medium-high.

4. Continue to stir until it thickens up.

5. Remove from the heat and pour through a mesh strainer to remove any egg bits.

6. Store in your refrigerator.

68.   Sugar-Free Maple Nut Fudge Serves 24

Ingredients:

8-ounce package of Mascarpone or Cream Cheese

1 teaspoon of Maple Extract

1 teaspoon of Stevia Glycerite

1 cup of Organic Butter

1/4 cup of Swerve

Options:

1 cup of Pecans or Walnuts

1/4 teaspoon of Ground Ginger

Directions:

1. In your small-sized saucepan, melt butter over a medium-high heat (heat until it turns brown, not black).

2. Add natural sweeteners until sweeteners dissolve and the mixture bubbles just a little.

3. Using a hand mixer on a low speed, add in extract and mascarpone.

4. Mix until well combined.

5. The mixture will not emulsify until it cools a little. I placed the mixture into my blender and combined until smooth which caused it to not separate. If you use a hand mixer, it keeps separating until cooled. So after it cools a bit, whip it together.

6. Stir in the nuts and ginger if using.

7. Place a piece of parchment in an 8x8 square baking pan. Pour your mixture into the pan lined with parchment. Refrigerate overnight, the mixture will thicken a lot. Remove from your pan, peel away parchment and cut into 1-inch cubes. Makes 24 servings.

Nutritional Value per serving:

Carbs: 19 grams

Calories: 110

69.   Sugar-Free Mounds Bars Serves 24

Ingredients:

1/3 cup of Organic Extra Virgin Coconut Oil

1/2 cup of Confectioner's Style Swerve

8 ounces of Dark Chocolate (85% Cacao)

1 cup of Unsweetened Organic Finely Shredded Coconut

1/3 cup of Organic Coconut Milk

Directions:

1. In your medium-sized saucepan, combine your coconut oil, coconut milk, and the sweetener.

2. Heat over a low heat, constantly mixing until the coconut oil has melted.

3. Add your shredded coconut and mix until well mixed.

4. Pour your mixture in a 9x5 inch silicone loaf pan. Press your mixture tightly and evenly to the bottom of your pan.

5. Refrigerate for 3 hours or until your mixture is solid.

6. Turn your pan upside down, gently press the bottom of your pan so that the solid mixture pops out.

7. Cut your mixture into bars.

8. Chop your chocolate into small-sized pieces, equal in size.

9. Melt 3 ounces of your chopped chocolate in a water bath or in a double boiler. Don't let the chocolate get too hot, heat it gently until it is melted, stirring occasionally.

10. Remove your melted chocolate from the heat. Add 1 ounce of chopped chocolate to your melted chocolate and mix occasionally to get a smooth mixture.

11. Dip your bars in the melted chocolate, put on parchment paper or on cooling rack and let the chocolate set.

12. When your chocolate coating is completely set, melt 3 ounces of the chopped chocolate in a water bath or in a double boiler. Don't let your chocolate get too hot, heat it gently until it is melted, stirring occasionally.

13. Remove the chocolate from your heat. Add the rest of your chopped chocolate (1 ounce) to your melted chocolate and mix occasionally to get a smooth mixture.

14. Dip your bars a second time in your melted chocolate, put on parchment paper or on cooling rack and allow your chocolate to set.

Nutritional Value per serving:

Net Carbs: 2.1 grams

Calories: 110

70.   Sugar-Free Panna Cotta Serves 4

Ingredients:

1 cup of Unsweetened Almond Milk

1 teaspoon of Vanilla Extract

1 cup of Heavy Cream

1/2 cup of Sugar-Free Raspberry Jam

1 sachet of Unflavored Gelatin

1/3 cup of Erythritol

1 tablespoon of Fresh Lemon Juice

Raspberries

Directions:

1. In your saucepan, combine the almond milk and heavy cream over a low flame.

2. Add your gelatin and erythritol. Allow to dissolve in your warm cream. Don't allow to boil.

3. Use your whisk to stir it together well.

4. Turn off heat and add your lemon juice and vanilla extract.

5. Grease 4 cups or ramekins. Spray with oil and pour your batter into each one evenly.

6. Cover your cup or ramekin with plastic wrap and place in refrigerator for a minimum of 2 hours.

7. Take out and run a knife around edges. Flip over onto a plate.

8. Top with your raspberry jam and fresh raspberries.

Nutritional Value per serving:

Calories: 131

Fat: 12 grams

Carbs: 11 grams

71.Vanilla Fat Bombs Serves 14

Ingredients:

1 cup of Unsalted Macadamia Nuts

1 Vanilla Bean or 2 teaspoon of Sugar-Free Vanilla Extract

1/4 cup of Virgin Coconut Oil

1/4 cup of Butter

Optional:

10 to 15 drops of Stevia Extract

2 tablespoons of Swerve

Directions:

1. Place your macadamia nuts into your blender and pulse until smooth.

2. Mix with your softened butter and coconut oil (room temperature or melted in a water bath).

3. Add your swerve, stevia, and vanilla bean.

4. Pour into your mini muffin forms or an ice cube tray. You should be able to fill each one about 1 1/2 tablespoons of your mixture to get 14 servings. Place in the refrigerator for approximately 30 minutes and let it solidify.

5. When done, keep refrigerated. Coconut oil and butter get soft at room temperature.

Nutritional Value per serving:

Net Carbs: 0.6 grams

Calories: 132

72.   White Chocolate Butter Pecan Bombs Serves 4

Ingredients:

2 tablespoons of Coconut Oil

1/4 teaspoon of Vanilla Extract

2 tablespoons of Powdered Erythritol

2 tablespoons of Butter

1/2 cup of Chopped Pecans

2 ounces of Cocoa Butter

Pinch of Stevia

Pinch of Salt

Directions:

1. Melt your coconut oil, cocoa butter, and butter together in a small-sized pan until melted. Then turn your heat off.

2. Stir in 2 tablespoons of powdered erythritol into your butter mixture until well combined.

3. Add a pinch of salt to bring out the sweetness.

4. Add a pinch of Stevia.

5. Add your vanilla extract.

6. Add a few chopped pecans into your silicone molds. Add around 3 to 4 pecans total to each mold. If you don't have pecans, walnuts and hazelnuts work well.

7. Pour your white chocolate mix evenly into the molds over your nuts and place in your freezer immediately.

8. Freeze for approximately 30 minutes.

Nutritional Value per serving:

Calories: 287

Carbs: 0.5 grams

Fat: 30 grams

73.   White Chocolate Raspberry Cheesecake Fluff

Ingredients:

2 ounces of Heavy Cream

1 teaspoon of Stevia Glycerite

8 ounces of Softened Cream Cheese

1 teaspoon of Low Sugar Raspberry Preserves

1 tablespoon of Da Vinci Sugar-Free White Chocolate Flavor Syrup

Directions:

1. Mix all your ingredients together and then whip it into a pudding-like consistency. Spoon mixture into small-sized serving cups and then refrigerate until it sets.

2.

74. Zabaglione w/ Meringues Serves 6

Ingredients:

6 Medium Organic Eggs (Yolks Divided From Whites)

3 Medium Organic Strawberries

1 stick of Organic Butter

4 tablespoons of Coconut Oil

1 gram of Powdered Stevia

2 teaspoons of Vanilla Extract (Divided)

1 cup of Heavy Whipping Cream

Zest of 1 Organic Lemon (Peeled w/ Potato Peeler)

Directions:

Meringues:

1. Pre-heat your oven to 200 degrees.

2. In your large-sized bowl place your egg whites, 1/2 of the stevia, and 1 teaspoon of vanilla extract.

3. With your hand mixer whip your egg whites, starting with a slow setting for about 30 seconds, until they become foamy, then on the fastest setting, until they get stiff and hold a peak.

4. Set to the side about 1/3 of your egg whites for later.

5. Line your cookie sheet with parchment paper.

6. Gently spoon your egg whites into a pastry bag with a large nozzle.

7. Squeeze little round mounds of egg white on your cookie sheet in a decorative fashion.

8. Set your cookie sheet in the oven and bake for approximately 3 hours with the door slightly ajar.

9. Meringues will be ready when they sound hollow when tapped.

Zabaglione:

1. Start melting your butter and coconut oil in a small-sized heat-resistant bowl, set in a small-sized saucepan of boiling water.

2. In your blender put your washed and trimmed strawberries, the zest of the lemon, the rest of your stevia and the vanilla extract.

3. Mix your eggs well, until smooth and foamy.

4. Add your strawberry mixture to them.

5. Once your butter has melted, slowly pour your egg yolk mix into your bowl, while mixing all the time with your hand mixer on the slowest setting.

6. Add the rest of your whipped egg whites in and mix gently.

7. Keep mixing the zabaglione, while holding the bowl, so it will not spin.

8. Cook for approximately 5 minutes, making sure that it does not stick to the sides of the bowl.

9. It should be light and frothy when done. Remove the bowl from the boiling water and set to the side.

Whipped Cream:

1. In a previously chilled bowl, pour your heavy cream.

2. Whip with your hand mixer on a high speed until stiff.

3. In a glass, layer the zabaglione with the meringue and top with whipped cream.

4. Serve immediately or pre-make and chill in the refrigerator.

Nutritional Value per serving:

Calories: 367

Fat: 36

75. Macadamia & Speculoos Biscotti Serves 10

Ingredients:

2 Large Eggs

3 ounces of Swerve Confectioners

7 ounces of Superfine Almond Flour

1 teaspoon of Xanthan Gum

1 teaspoon of Baking Powder

2 1/2 ounces of Dry Roasted Macadamia Nuts

1 teaspoon of Vanilla Bean Paste

2 ounces of Melted Salted Butter

1 tablespoon of Speculoos Spice Blend

Directions:

1. Preheat your oven to 325 degrees. In your bowl, combine your almond flour, sweetener, baking powder, xanthan gum, vanilla paste, macadamia, and spice blend. Mix together well.

2. In your separate bowl, melt your butter. Add your eggs. Beat well.

3. Add your butter and egg mixture to the dry ingredients.

4. Mix well and form into a dough.

5. Transfer your dough to a work surface, pat, and form into an even, flattened, oblong or square-ish shaped log. Note that the dough is sticky. To help with the shaping, dust hands with almond flour.

6. Transfer your dough to a parchment lined sheet tray and bake for approximately 30 minutes or until firm, lightly golden, and top is slightly cracked. Remove from your oven. Set to the side to cool, approximately 15 minutes.

7. When cool, slice your loaf into half inch thick slices.

8. Preheat your oven to 250 degrees.

9. Line slices on a parchment lined sheet tray. Bake for approximately 15 minutes. Flip your slices and bake for another 15 minutes.

10. Turn your oven off. Allow the the biscotti to cool in your oven until crisp, crunchy, and dry. Store in an airtight container.

Nutritional Value per serving:

Calories: 190

Net Carbs: 2.7 grams

Protein: 5 grams

76. Macaroon Fat Bombs Serves 10

Ingredients:

1/4 cup of Organic Almond Flour

1/2 cup of Shredded Coconut

2 tablespoons of Swerve

3 Egg Whites

1 tablespoon of Vanilla Extract

1 tablespoon of Coconut Oil

Directions:

1. In your bowl mix almond flour, coconut, and swerve until well blended.

2. Melt your coconut oil in a small-sized saucepan and add your vanilla extract to it.

3. In the meantime, chill your medium-sized bowl in your freezer for mounting the egg whites.

4. Add your melted coconut oil to the flour mix and blend well.

5. Put your egg whites in your chilled bowl and whisk until stiff, very foamy holding stiff peaks.

6. Incorporate your egg whites into your flour mix, trying to not over mix and to preserve some of the volume from the eggs whites.

7. Spoon your mixture onto a cookie sheet, or into muffin cups.

8. Bake at 400 degrees for 8 minutes or until macaroons start to brown on top.
9. Remove from your oven and allow it to cool before removing from the cookie sheet.
Nutritional Value per serving:
Calories: 46
Net Carbs: 0.5 grams

77.   Matcha Skillet Souffle Serves 1

Ingredients:
3 Large Eggs
7 Whole Raspberries
1 tablespoon of Butter
1 tablespoon of Unsweetened Cocoa Powder
1 tablespoon of Matcha Powder
1 teaspoon of Vanilla Extract
2 tablespoons of Swerve Confectioners
1/4 cup of Whipped Cream
1 tablespoon of Coconut Oil
Directions:
1. Set your oven to broil, and preheat a cast iron pan over a medium heat. Separate your eggs into yolks and whites.
2. Whip your whites with 1 tablespoon of Swerve confectioners. Once peaks form add in your matcha powder Continue to whip until the peaks become stiff. (I've also done this by adding everything at once to a stand mixer, but it failed to whip with a hand mixer.)
3. Use a fork to break up the yolks. Mix in the vanilla then add a small amount of the whipped whites. Carefully fold the rest of the whites into your yolk mixture.
4. Add your tablespoon of butter to the cast iron pan. Allow it to melt then add the souffle mixture to the pan. Turn the heat to low then place the raspberries on top. Allow it to cook until your eggs puff up and feel set if you carefully tap the top.
5. Move your skillet to the oven and watch it carefully. Remove once the top starts to brown. If you leave it in too long it may turn quite dark or burn.
6. Melt your coconut oil then whisk in your cocoa powder and remaining tablespoon of Swerve confectioners. Drizzle across the top. Serve with 1/4 cup of whipped cream.
Nutritional Value per serving:
Calories: 578
Net Carbs: 5 grams
Fat: 51 grams

78.   Mexican Chocolate Pudding Serves 2

Ingredients:
1 tablespoon of Coconut Milk
1 teaspoon of Ceylon Cinnamon
1 Avocado
2 1/2 tablespoons of Raw Cocoa Powder
1 tablespoon of Coconut Milk
1/16 teaspoon of Ground Cayenne Pepper
1/2 teaspoon of Pure Vanilla Extract
1 tablespoon of Sweetener
Pinch of Stevia
Pinch of Pink Himalayan Sea Salt
Directions:
1. Cut and pit your avocado. Blend in food processor until smooth.
2. Add your coconut milk, vanilla extract, and cocoa powder. Blend it until it is smooth.

3. Add your cinnamon, sweetener, ground cayenne pepper, and Stevia.
4. Blend until smooth. Get rid of all your chunks.
5. Sprinkle with sea salt.
Nutritional Value per serving:
Calories: 180
Protein: 3 grams
Fat: 15 grams
Carbs: 3.5 grams

79.   Mini Cheesecakes Serves 8

Ingredients:
Cheesecake:
1 Egg
1/4 cup of Erythritol
8 ounces of Cream Cheese
1/2 teaspoon of Vanilla Extract
1/2 teaspoon of Lemon Juice
Pinch of Salt
Crust:
1/2 cup of Almond Meal
2 tablespoons of Butter
Directions:
1. Preheat your oven to 350 degrees.
2. To make your crust, melt your butter until it is liquid and then mix with your almond meal.
3. Take a teaspoon of dough at a time and press into bottom of your muffin tin. You can line your pan with cupcake liners to make removal easy.
4. Bake your crusts approximately 5 minutes at 350 degrees. Should be crispy and slightly brown.
5. Beat your cream cheese with your electric hand mixer until it is creamy. Add in lemon, vanilla extract, erythritol, and egg. Beat until well combined.
6. Fill all the crust bottomed muffin tin cups. Do so evenly and nearly to the top.
7. Bake for approximately 15 minutes at 350 degrees. Cheesecakes should be a little jiggly.
8. Allow it to cool.
9. Slide knife around outer edges of each cup to loosen.
Nutritional Value per serving:
Calories: 176
Protein: 4 grams
Fat: 16 grams
Carbs: 2 grams

80.   Mint Chocolate Chip Ice Cream Serves 4

Ingredients:
1 cup of Heavy Cream
1/2 teaspoon of Liquid Stevia Extract
1/2 cup of Light Cream
1 Square Dark Chocolate (Optional)
1/2 teaspoon of Vanilla (Optional)
Several drops of Peppermint Extract (Optional)
Several drops of Green Food Coloring (Optional)
Directions:
1. Place your ice cream bowl in your freezer 4 to 12 hours ahead of time.
2. Place all of your ingredients in ice cream bowl except the chocolate.

3. Whisk together well.
4. Place in your freezer for approximately 5 minutes.
5. Set up your ice cream maker and add in liquid.
6. Make ice cream according to your machine's instructions. A few minutes before ice cream sets, add in your chocolate shavings.
7. Store in air tight container and place back in the freezer.
8. Allow to freeze.
Nutritional Value per serving:
Calories: 295
Fat: 31 grams
Carbs: 3.5 grams

81. Mocha Peppermint Fat Bombs Serves 16

Ingredients:
3/4 cup of Melted Coconut Butter
3 tablespoons of Melted Coconut Oil
1/4 teaspoon of Peppermint Extract
3 tablespoons of Hemp Seeds
2 teaspoons of Instant Coffee Powder
2 tablespoons of Organic Cocoa Powder
5 to 8 drops of Liquid Stevia
Directions:
1. Mix together your melted coconut butter, 1 tablespoon of coconut oil, hemp seeds, and peppermint extract.
2. Pour into molds about 3/4 of the way.
3. Refrigerate until firm.
4. Stir together 2 tablespoons of melted coconut oil, cocoa powder, instant coffee, and stevia.
5. Drizzle on top of your fat bombs.
6. Refrigerate again until completely hardened.
7. Pop out of your molds and transfer to an airtight container.
8. Store in your refrigerator or freezer.
Nutritional Value per serving:
Carbs: 4 grams
Calories: 121

82.   No Bake Lemon Cheesecake

Ingredients:
8 ounces of Softened Cream Cheese
2 ounces of Heavy Cream
1 teaspoon of Stevia Glycerite
1 tablespoon of Lemon Juice
1 teaspoon of Vanilla Flavoring
1 teaspoon of Splenda
Directions:
1. Mix all your ingredients together and then whip it into a pudding-like consistency. Spoon mixture into small serving cups and then refrigerate till it sets.

83.   No Flour Chocolate Cake Serves 8

Ingredients:
3 Eggs
1 cup of Swerve Erythritol (separated into 1/2 cup, 1/4 cup, 1/4 cup)
1/2 cup of Cocoa Powder

1/2 cup of Butter
4 ounces of Unsweetened Baker's Chocolate
1/2 teaspoon of Salt
1 teaspoon of Vanilla Extract
Directions:
1. Preheat your oven to 300 degrees. Set up your double boiler to melt your butter and baker's chocolate together. If no boiler use your pan over a low heat.
2. Once they are both melted, combine them both together. Add in 1/2 cup of erythritol and stir well over a low flame until it is dissolved.
3. Separate 3 eggs and beat your eggs whites until foamy. Add 1/4 cup of erythritol slowly while beating your egg whites. Should form stiff peaks and turn glossy.
4. Clean your beaters and beat your 3 egg yolks. Slowly add in the last 1/4 cup of erythritol. Yolks should turn pale yellow and double in volume.
5. Add your chocolate mixture to egg yolks. Stir well.
6. Add your cocoa powder. Stir well. Add your salt and vanilla.
7. Add a third of your egg whites and fold in gently. Repeat this process until all your eggs whites have been added and folded in.
8. Spray your springform pan with cooking oil. Pour in your chocolate batter. Bake for approximately 35 minutes.
9. Dust with powdered erythritol.
Nutritional Value per serving:
Calories: 240
Carbs: 2 grams
Fat: 21 grams

84.   Nutella Brownies Serves 4

Ingredients:
4 Eggs
4 tablespoons of Erythritol
1 Cup of Nutella
Directions:
1. Preheat your oven to 350 degrees.
2. Place your Nutella in a microwave for approximately 15-second intervals, stirring until it gets really soft.
3. Crack your eggs and mix with electric mixer until they've tripled in volume and become a lighter yellow color. Should take approximately 5 to 8 minutes.
4. Combine your Nutella and eggs. Whisk until it is combined. Add your erythritol.
5. Add your mixture to ramekins. Put your ramekins on a cookie sheet. Bake for approximately 25 to 30 minutes.
6. Allow it to cool.
Nutritional Value per serving:
Calories: 396
Protein: 12 grams
Fat: 35 grams
Carbs: 4 grams

85.   Nutella Sundae Serves 2

Ingredients:
4 scoops of Low-Carb Ice Cream
2 tablespoons of Homemade Nutella
2 Strawberries
Sprinkles

Whipped Cream
Directions:
1. Mix it all together.
2. Place in your bowl.
3. Add your toppings.
Nutritional Value per serving:
Calories: 191
Protein: 4 grams
Fat: 14 grams
Carbs: 10 grams

86.   Nutty Coconut Fat Bombs Serves 15
Ingredients:
1 1/2 cups of Walnuts
2 tablespoons of Almond Butter
1/4 cup of Coconut Butter + 1 tablespoon
1/2 cup of Shredded Coconut
2 tablespoons of Chia Seeds
2 tablespoons of Flax Meal
1/2 teaspoon of Vanilla Bean Powder
2 tablespoons of Hemp Seeds
2 tablespoons of Cacao Nibs
1 teaspoon of Cinnamon
1/4 teaspoon of Kosher Salt
Chocolate Drizzle:
1/2 teaspoon of Coconut Oil
1 ounce of Bittersweet or Unsweetened Chocolate (Chopped)
Directions:
1. In the bowl of your food processor, combine all of your ingredients except for the cacao nibs. Pulse for about 1 to 2 minutes, until the mixture starts to break down. It will first become powdery and will stick together, but still be crumbly.
2. Keep processing until the oils start to release a bit and the mixture sticks together easily - just be careful not to over process or you'll have nut butter. If your mixture seems dry and if you're not using the maple syrup, you may need the extra tablespoon of coconut butter to help it come together. Once your mixture is sticking together well, pulse in your cacao nibs to incorporate them.
3. Use a small-sized cookie scoop or a tablespoon scoop to divide the mixture into equal pieces. Use your hands to roll into balls and place on a plate.
4. If desired, make your chocolate drizzle by melting the chocolate and coconut oil together in your microwave for 30 seconds to 1 minute, or until it's completely melted. Drizzle over the balls and place in the refrigerator or freezer to firm up.
5. Store in an airtight container zip-top bag in the refrigerator or freezer.
Nutritional Value per serving:
Calories: 164
Fat: 14 grams

87.   Panna Cotta & Cream Hearts Serves 8
Ingredients:
Panna Cotta:
2 cups of Organic Heavy Whipping Cream
2 teaspoons of Gelatin
2 tablespoons of Swerve

1 tablespoon of Vanilla Extract
Cream:
2 cups of Organic Heavy Whipping Cream
2 teaspoons of Gelatin
6 Organic or Pastured Egg Yolks
4 tablespoons of Swerve
1 tablespoon of Vanilla Extract
1 teaspoon of Butter (For Greasing)
Zest of 1 Organic Lemon
Decoration:
2 tablespoons of Chopped Roasted Hazelnuts
Directions:
Panna Cotta:
1. Sprinkle your gelatin on the cream and stir well.
2. In your small-sized saucepan warm the cream on a low flame stirring constantly until all the gelatin is dissolved.
3. Add your Swerve and vanilla extract and keep stirring for another minute. Do not let the cream come to a boil. After a minute turn off your flame and allow it to sit for about a minute.
4. Grease your springform with your butter.
5. Pour half of your panna cotta mixture in the bottom of your springform and allow it to cool.
6. Keep the remaining panna cotta fluid by keeping it in a warm oven (170 degrees).
Cream:
1. Mix your cream and gelatin and stir together well.
2. In the same small-sized saucepan start warming the cream on a low flame.
3. In your medium-sized bowl, whisk your egg yolks with Swerve and your lemon zest until they are well-emulsified (they should be whitish and fluffy).
4. Slowly add a cup of warm cream to your egg mixture, whisking the whole time and being careful not to get lumps.
5. Once your mix is fluid and blended with the cup of cream add it to your saucepan carefully, constantly whisking.
6. Bring your mix to a simmer, keep whisking, and cook for approximately 3 minutes, until your cream starts to thicken.
7. Allow it to cool for approximately 5 minutes, whisking occasionally.
8. Once your panna cotta layer has solidified at the top, pour your cooled cream into your springform pan distributing it evenly, the cream should be pretty thick and solid but still spreadable.
9. Pour the last half of your panna cotta on top and allow it to cool.
10. Once cooled to room temperature you can put your springform in the refrigerator for 3 hours or overnight.
11. Remove border from your springform after loosening the sides with a pointed knife.
12. Cut as many hearts as possible into your panna cotta and cream.
13. Remove the hearts with a flat spatula and a knife, cutting off the extra dough.
14. Serve cold with a sprinkle of toasted hazelnuts.
Nutritional Value per serving:
Calories: 467
Fat: 53 grams

88. Peanut Butter Chocolate Truffles
Ingredients:
6 ounces of Sugar-Free Chocolate
1 1/2 cups of Powdered Erythritol
4 tablespoons of Melted Butter
1 cup of Peanut Butter

Directions:
1. Melt your butter.
2. Mix your peanut butter, powdered erythritol, and melted butter together.
3. Scoop out your 2 tablespoons of mixture and roll out into small-sized balls. Lay on your baking sheet lined with parchment paper. Chill in your refrigerator for approximately 30 minutes.
4. Melt your chocolate in a small-sized bowl for approximately 10 to 20 seconds in your microwave. Stir it well.
5. Place one of your truffles in your bowl at a time and rotate it with a spoon so that chocolate covers every side. Take out and allow excess chocolate to fall off.
6. Place back on your baking sheet lined with parchment paper and place in refrigerator for another hour to chill.
Nutritional Value per serving:
Calories: 200
Carbs: 5 grams
Protein: 6 grams
Fat: 17 grams

89. Chocolate Coconut Candies Serves 20

Ingredients:
Chocolate Topping:
1 ounce of Unsweetened Chocolate
1 1/2 ounces of Cocoa Butter
1/4 cup of Cocoa Powder
1/4 teaspoon of Vanilla Extract
1/4 cup of Powdered Swerve Sweetener
Coconut Candies:
1/2 cup of Coconut Butter
3 tablespoons of Powdered Swerve Sweetener
1/2 cup of Coconut Oil
1/2 cup of Unsweetened Shredded Coconut
Directions:
1. For the candies, line your mini-muffin pan with 20 mini paper liners.
2. Combine your coconut butter and coconut oil in a small-sized saucepan over a low heat. Stir until melted and smooth and then stir in your shredded coconut and sweetener until combined.
3. Divide your mixture among prepared mini muffin cups and freeze until firm, approximately 30 minutes.
4. For the chocolate coating, combine your cocoa butter and unsweetened chocolate together in a bowl set over a pan of simmering water (do not let the bottom of the bowl touch the water). Stir until melted.
5. Stir in your sifted powdered sweetener, then stir in your cocoa powder, until smooth.
6. Remove from your heat and stir in your vanilla extract.
7. Spoon your chocolate topping over a chilled coconut candies and allow it to set, approximately 15 minutes.
8. Candies can be stored on your counter for up to a week.
Nutritional Value per serving:
Net Carbs: 1 gram
Calories: 240

90. Chocolate Covered Maple Pecan Bacon Serves 13

Ingredients:

Bacon Base:

13 slices of Bacon

1 tablespoon of Maple Extract

2 tablespoons of Erythritol

Coating:

1/4 cup of Chopped Roasted Pecans

4 tablespoons of Unsweetened Cocoa Powder

15 drops of Liquid Stevia

2 tablespoons of Erythritol

Directions:

1. Preheat your oven to 400 degrees. Lay your 13 slices of bacon onto a baking sheet lined with foil.

2. Sprinkle 1 tablespoon of erythritol and 1 1/2 teaspoon of maple extract over one side of the bacon and rub it in.

3. Flip your bacon onto the other side and do the same thing. Rub everything in well.

4. Bake your bacon for approximately 40 to 50 minutes until crisp.

5. Once your bacon is finished, set to the side for 5 minutes to allow it to cool for a moment.

6. In a container, render your bacon fat by tipping cooking sheet at an angle. This should get you about 5 tablespoons of bacon fat.

7. Add 4 tablespoons of cocoa powder, 2 tablespoons of erythritol, and 15 drops of liquid stevia to the bacon grease and mix together well.

8. Transfer your chocolate mixture to a different container so that you can dip the bacon inside. Submerge all the bacon into your chocolate and transfer to a sheet of parchment paper. Sprinkle 1/4 cup of chopped pecans over the bacon before chocolate dries.

9. Put the chocolate covered bacon into your refrigerator for at least 5 hours.

Nutritional Value per serving:

Calories: 75

Net Carbs: 0.75 grams

91. Chocolate Covered Strawberries

Ingredients:

1/2 pound of Fresh Strawberries

2 ounces of Chocolate Chips

1 tablespoon of Coconut Oil

2 tablespoons of Coconut Butter

Directions:

1. Melt your chocolate chips. Stir well.

2. Remove from any heat and add in your coconut oil and coconut butter until everything is melted. Move to a small-sized bowl.

3. Dry your strawberries. Grab by stem and dip into the chocolate.

4. Place your chocolate strawberries on a baking sheet lined with parchment paper and refrigerate for approximately 1 hour.

92.   Chocolate Strawberry Mousse Serves 1

Ingredients:

1/3 cup of Heavy Whipping Cream

1 Strawberry

4 Drops of EZ-Sweet

1/2 Scoop of Chocolate Whey Powder

2.5 grams of Unsweetened Cocoa

Flakes of 90% Chocolate

Directions:

1, Measure your cream into a container.
2. Add your EZ-Sweet.
3. Add your strawberry.
4. Add your powder.
5. Add your chocolate flakes.
6. Mix 1 to 2 minutes till stiff.
Nutritional Value per serving:
330 Calories
Protein: 10 grams
Fat: 33 grams
Carbs: 12 grams

93. Cinnamon Butter Fat Bombs

Ingredients:
1 tablespoon of Cinnamon
1 pound of Grass-Fed Salted Butter
1 1/2 teaspoons of Vanilla Extract
1/4 cup of Honey
Directions:
1. Allow your butter to soften.
2. Add your butter, cinnamon, honey, and vanilla extract to your food processor. Process for a couple of minutes to mix your ingredients and achieve a slightly whipped taste. Stop your food processor as necessary to scrape down the bowl and reincorporate ingredients.
3. Spoon your butter mixture into silicone molds. Alternatively, you can line a cutting board or flat surface with your parchment paper and then spoon dollops of your butter mixture onto your parchment paper.
4. Freeze for an hour or two, then remove from your parchment paper or molds and store in a container in your freezer.

94. Cinnamon Coconut Peanut Butter Cookies Serves 15

Ingredients:
1 cup of Peanut Butter
1 Egg
1/2 teaspoon of Vanilla Extract
1/4 cup of Butter
1/2 cup of Erythritol
2 tablespoons of Shredded Coconut
1 tablespoon of Cinnamon
Pinch of Salt
Directions:
1. Preheat your oven to 350 degrees. Beat together your butter, peanut butter, erythritol, and egg.
2. Add your cinnamon, shredded coconut, salt and fold it all in together.
3. Roll into balls about 1 1/2 inches in diameter. Lay out on a baking sheet lined with parchment paper.
4. Sprinkle with your shredded coconut.
5. Bake approximately for 15 minutes. Edges should become golden colored.
6. Allow it to cool.
Nutritional Value per serving:
Calories: 140
Protein: 4 grams
Fat: 12 grams

Carbs: 2 grams

95.   Clean Almond Butter Fat Bombs Serves 12
Ingredients:
1/4 cup of Almond Flour
2 tablespoons of Mesquite Meal
1 cup of Almond Butter
1 tablespoon of Melted Unrefined Virgin Coconut Oil
1/2 teaspoon of Vanilla Extract
1/4 cup of Coconut Flakes
4 Dates
Directions:
1. Combine all of your ingredients in your food processor.
2. Roll out 1-ounce balls and place them on your parchment-lined baking sheet. Note: If your almond butter has a runny consistency, throw your combined ingredients in the refrigerator or freezer before rolling them into individual balls.
3. Roll your balls into the topping of your choice.
4. Store in your refrigerator or freezer.

96.   Coconut Blackberry Fat Bombs Serves 16
Ingredients:
1 cup of Coconut Butter
1 tablespoon of Lemon Juice
1/4 teaspoon of Vanilla Powder or 1/2 teaspoon of Vanilla Extract
1 cup of Coconut Oil
1/2 teaspoon of Sweet Leaf Stevia Drops
1/2 cup of Fresh or Frozen Blackberries
Directions:
1. Place your coconut butter, coconut oil, and blackberries (if frozen) in a pot and heat over a medium heat until well combined.
2. In your food processor or small blender, add your coconut oil mix and remaining ingredients. Process until smooth. Separation may occur if coconut oil mixture is too hot. If using fresh berries, there is no need to cook them with the coconut oil and butter.
3. Spread out into a small-sized pan lined with parchment paper (I used a 6x6-inch container)
4. Refrigerate for one hour or until your mix has hardened.
5. Remove from your container and cut into squares.
6. Store covered in your refrigerator.
Nutritional Value per serving:
Carbs: 3 grams
Fat: 19 grams
Calories: 170

97.   Coconut Macaroons Serves 10
Ingredients:
4 Egg Whites
4 1/2 teaspoons of Water
1 teaspoon of Vanilla
2 cups of Unsweetened Coconut
1/2 teaspoon of EZ-Sweet
Directions:
1. Combine your egg whites and liquids.
2. Add your coconut and mix together.

3. Spread on your greased pie pan.
4. Preheat your oven to 375 degrees. When you put in your macaroons reduce heat to 325 degrees and bake for approximately 14 minutes.
Nutritional Value per serving:
Calories: 88
Protein: 2 grams
Fat: 8 grams
Carbs: 3 grams

98.   Coconut Raspberry Slice Serves 20

Ingredients:
Biscuit Layer:
1 Large Egg
2 cups of Almond Meal
1 tablespoon of Butter (Room Temperature)
1/2 teaspoon of Baking Soda
Coconut Layer:
1 cup of Unsweetened Coconut Milk (Canned)
1/3 cup of Powdered Erythritol
1/4 cup of Coconut Oil
1 teaspoon of Vanilla Bean Powder
3 cups of Unsweetened Desiccated Coconut
Pinch of Sea Salt
Raspberry Layer:
1 cup of Raspberries
3 tablespoons of Chia Seeds
1 teaspoon of Powdered Erythritol
2 tablespoons of Water
Chocolate Layer:
4 ounces of 85% Dark Chocolate
Directions:
1. Preheat your oven to 350 degrees. Combine all your biscuit layer ingredients in a bowl and mix until your dough forms.
2. Line an 8×8 inch baking dish or brownie pan with your parchment paper. Evenly press your biscuit dough into the dish to form the base. Bake in the oven for approximately 15 minutes, until lightly browned and cooked through. Allow it to cool.
3. Make your raspberry layer by adding all of your ingredients into a small-sized pan and stir over a low heat. Break up your raspberries as they cook so a jam forms. Keep stirring for around 5 minutes, until thickened. Allow it to cool.
4. On a medium heat mix your coconut milk and coconut oil until combined.
5. Mix all of your remaining ingredients for the coconut layer together. Add your coconut milk and oil mixture to the dry ingredients and combine well.
6. Add your coconut mixture to your cooled biscuit base and spread evenly. Place in your freezer until set (around 1 hour). Once the coconut layer is hard, spread the raspberry layer over the top of it and return to the freezer to set (around 1 hour).
7. Break your chocolate bar into small-sized pieces, then place in a suitable bowl and melt in your microwave (approximately 3 minutes). Pour your chocolate onto the raspberry layer and return to the freezer to set.
8. Remove from your freezer around 30 minutes before serving. The slices can be stored in the refrigerator for around a week or in the freezer for around 3 months.
Nutritional Value per serving:
Calories: 240
Net Carbs: 3.5 grams

Protein: 4.5 grams

99. Coconut Strawberry-Filled Fat Bombs Serves 15

Ingredients:

1/3 cup of Coconut Butter

1/3 cup of Diced Fresh Strawberries

1 tablespoons of Unsweetened Shredded Coconut

1/2 tablespoon of Cocoa Powder

1/3 cup of Coconut Oil + 1 tablespoon

8 to 10 drops of Liquid Stevia

Directions:

1. In your bain-marie, add your coconut butter, 1/3 cup of coconut oil, cocoa powder, and a few drops of liquid stevia. Heat until fully melted.

2. Meanwhile, in your small-sized frying pan, add your fresh strawberries and a few spoonfuls of water. Cook over a medium heat until soft. Mash with a fork. Add the berries to a blender with 1 tablespoon of melted coconut oil and a few more drops of liquid stevia. Blend until smooth.

3. Fill your molds with the melted coconut mixture. Add about 1 teaspoon of the strawberry mixture into each mold. Sprinkle with a few shreds of unsweetened coconut.

4. Place in your refrigerator until fully hardened; at least a couple of hours or overnight. Pop out of the molds and store in an air-tight container in the refrigerator.

Nutritional Value per serving:

Net Carbs: 1 gram

Calories: 106

100. Coconut White Chocolate Fudge Serves 24

Ingredients:

4 ounces of Cacao Butter

1 teaspoon of Coconut Liquid Stevia

1/2 cup of Vanilla Protein Powder

1/2 cup of Coconut Oil

1 cup of Coconut Butter

15-ounce can of Coconut Milk

1 teaspoon of Vanilla Extract

Pinch of Salt

Optional:

Unsweetened Coconut Flake

Directions:

1. Melt your cacao butter in your saucepan over a low heat.

2. Stir in your coconut milk, coconut oil, and coconut butter.

3. Continue to stir until completely smooth, no lumps.

4. Turn off your heat and whisk in protein powder, vanilla extract, stevia, and salt.

5. Pour your mixture into a parchment lined 8x8 pan.

6. Sprinkle with coconut flakes if desired.

7. Refrigerate for 4 hours or overnight.

8. Does not need to be kept refrigerated for storage.

Nutritional Value per serving:

Net Carbs: 1.2 grams

Calories: 175

101. Coffee Cake Cinnamon Collagen Fat Bombs Serves 12

Ingredients:

1/4 cup of Almond Butter
1/2 cup of Coconut Oil
1 tablespoon of Instant Coffee
1 packet of Vanilla Collagen
1 teaspoon of Cinnamon
Directions:
1. In your small-sized saucepan heat coconut oil and almond butter on low until melted.
2. Microwave your coconut oil for approximately 30 seconds until melted.
3. Stir together all of your ingredients.
4. Pour into an 8x8 pan, mini muffin tins, or silicone/plastic candy molds. Freeze until firm.

102.   Cream Cheese Peanut Butter Fat Bombs

Ingredients:
3/4 cup of Softened Peanut Butter
4 ounces of Softened Cream Cheese
2 tablespoons of Softened Butter
1 tablespoon of Lemon Juice
3/4 cup of Almond Flour
1/4 cup of Swerve Icing
Directions:
1. Line 12 mini muffin tins with your paper liners and set to the side. You can also use your ice cube tray.
2. In your medium-sized bowl, combine your softened cream cheese, butter, and peanut butter until completely smooth. Add your almond flour, lemon juice, and sweetener and whisk until combined. Evenly distribute into the prepared muffin tins.
3. Place in your freezer for at least 1 hour. Once frozen, transfer the fat bombs to a Ziploc bag for better storing. Keep them in the freezer for up to 3 months.

103.   Heroic Orange And Coconut Creamsicles

Servings: 6
Prep time: 10 minutes + 3 hours chill time

Ingredients:
½ c of coconut oil
½ c of heavy whipping cream
4 oz of cream cheese
1 tsp of orange mix
10 drops of liquid stevia

Instructions:
1. Take a bowl and add the listed ingredients
2. Use an immersion blender and blend the mixture well
3. Take a silicone tray and add the mixture
4. Let it freeze for 2-3 hours
   5. Serve and enjoy!

Nutritional Value per serving:
Calories: 176 | Fat: 20 g | Carbohydrates: 0.7 g | Net Carbohydrates: 0.5 g | Fiber: 1 g | Protein: 0.8 g

104.   Authentic Low-Carb Pumpkin Mousse

Servings: 6
Prep time: 5-10 minutes

Ingredients:
1 pack unflavored gelatin
1 tbsp of cold water
2 tbsp of boiling water
8 oz of cream cheese, soft
5 tbsp Truvia
1 and ½ tsp of pumpkin pie spice
15 oz of pumpkin puree
1 c of whipped cream

Instructions:
1. Sprinkle gelatin over 1 tablespoon of cold water in a small sized bowl
2. Add 2 tablespoons of boiling water and gently stir until gelatin is dissolved
3. Add cream cheese alongside sweetener and mix until blended
4. Blend in pumpkin spice mix
5. Stir in gelatin and mix well
6. Fold in whipped cream and beat until the mixture is fluffy
7. Spoon the mixture into serving dishes and chill
8. **ENJOY!**

Nutritional Value per serving:
Calories: 165 | Fat: 14 g | Carbohydrates: 5 g | Net Carbohydrates: 3 g | Fiber: 1 g | Protein: 3 g

105.   Sugar-Free Cheesecake Mousse

Servings: 5
Prep time: 5 minutes + 2 hours chill time

Ingredients:
8z of soft cream
1/3 c of powdered Erythritol
1/8 tsp of stevia
1 and ½ tsp of vanilla extract
¼ tsp of lemon extract
1 c of heavy cream

Instructions:
1. Take a bowl and beat in cream cheese until you have a smooth mixture
2. Add vanilla, Erythritol, stevia, lemon extract and mix well
3. Take another bowl and beat in heavy cream until you have a nice mixture
4. Fold in half of the whipped cream into cheese mixture and stir
5. Fold other half and mix well
6. Beat the whole mixture using a hand mixer on high (until fluffy)
7. Let it chill for 2 hours
8. Serve with a topping of Keto-Friendly berries
9. **ENJOY!**

Nutritional Value per serving:

Calories: 269 | Fat: 27 g | Carbohydrates: 12 g | Net Carbohydrates: 6 g | Fiber: 2 g | Protein: 4 g

106.   Premium Cookie Dough

Servings: 6
Prep time: 10 minutes

Ingredients:
¾ c of heavy cream
¼ c of stevia
¾ c of coconut flour
½ c of melted butter
½ tsp of vanilla extract
¼ tsp of salt
¼ c of sugar-free chocolate chips

Instructions:
1. Take a large sized bowl and add cream, sweetener, coconut flour, salt, butter. Vanilla and blend the mixture well
2. Stir in chocolate chips and mix
3. Scoop the dough into bite-sized portions and enjoy!

Nutritional Value per serving:
Calories: 179 | Fat: 15 g | Carbohydrates: 8 g | Net Carbohydrates: 5 g | Fiber: 1 g | Protein: 2 g

107.   Mesmerizing Keto Butter-Cream

Servings: 6
Prep time: 10 minutes

Ingredients:
2 oz of unsalted butter
2 tsp of vanilla extract
1 and ½ tsp of coconut aminos

Instructions:
1. Take a small saucepan and place it over medium heat
2. Add 2 ounce of butter and melt it
3. Once browned, add coconut aminos
4. Pour the browned butter into a beaker and add the remaining butter
5. Use an immersion blender to blend the whole mix
6. Add your desired flavor on top and serve!

Nutritional Value per serving:
Calories: 294 | Fat: 26 g | Carbohydrates: 10 g | Net Carbohydrates: 6 g | Fiber: 1 g | Protein: 1 g

108.   Friendly Vanilla Custard

Servings: 6
Prep time: 10 minutes

Ingredients:

6 whole egg yolks
½ c of unsweetened almond milk
1 tsp of vanilla extract
4 tbsp of melted coconut oil
1 tsp of stevia

Instructions:
1. Whisk egg yolks, almond milk, vanilla and stevia in a medium sized metal bowl
2. Slowly mix in melted coconut oil and stir
3. Place the bowl over a saucepan of simmer water
4. Keep whisking the mixture vigorously until thick
5. Use a thermometer to register the temperature, once it has reached 140 degrees Fahrenheit, keep it steady for 3 minutes
6. Remove the custard from the water bath and serve chilled!

Nutritional Value per serving:
Calories: 204 | Fat: 18 g | Carbohydrates: 8 g | Net Carbohydrates: 4 g | Fiber: 1 g | Protein: 5 g

109.   Awesome Coffee Popsicles

Servings: 4
Prep time: 2 hours

Ingredients:
2 tbsp chocolate chips, sugar-free
2 c coffee, brewed and cold
¾ c heavy whip cream
2 tsp natural sweetener

Instructions:
1. Blend in heavy whip cream, sweetened and coffee in a blender
2. Mix well
3. Pour mix into popsicle molds and add a few chocolate chips
4. Let it freeze for 2 hours
5. Serve and enjoy!

Nutritional Value per serving:
Calories: 105 | Fat: 10 g | Carbohydrates: 2 g | Net Carbohydrates: 1 g | Fiber: 1 g | Protein: 2 g

110.   Simple Icy Berry Popsicles

Servings: 2
Prep time: 2 hours

Ingredients:
2 c coconut cream
2 tsp of stevia
¼ c of mixed blackberries and blueberries

Instructions:
1. Blend the listed ingredients in a blender until smooth

2. Pour mix into popsicle molds and let them chill for 2 hours
   3. Serve and enjoy!

Nutritional Value per serving:
Calories: 165 | Fat: 17 g | Carbohydrates: 2 g | Net Carbohydrates: 1 g | Fiber: 1 g | Protein: 1 g

111.   The Pecan And Mascarpone Bowl

Servings: 2
Prep time: 5 minutes

Ingredients:
1 c pecans, chopped
1 drop liquid stevia
¼ c of mascarpone
30 dark chocolate chips (check for Keto-Friendliness)
6 strawberries, sliced

Instructions:
1. Divide the pecans between dessert bowls
2. Take a small bowl and add sweetener and mascarpone cheese
3. Take a serving bowl and add nuts
4. Top with a dollop of sweetened mascarpone
5. Sprinkle chocolate chips and top with strawberries
6. **ENJOY!**

Nutritional Value per serving:
Calories: 462 | Fat: 47 g | Carbohydrates: 6 g | Net Carbohydrates: 4g | Fiber: 1 g | Protein: 6 g
|

112.   Easy "Fudgesicles"

Servings: 4
Prep time: 2 hours 5 minutes

Ingredients:
2 tbsp of cocoa powder, unsweetened
2 tbsp of chocolate chips, sugar-free
2 tsp natural sweetener, such as stevia
¾ c heavy whip cream

Instructions:
1. Take a blender and add your listed ingredients
2. Blend until smooth
3. Pour the mixture into popsicle molds and let them chill for 2 hours
   4. Serve and enjoy!

Nutritional Value per serving:
Calories: 193 | Fat: 20G | Carbohydrates: 4g | Net Carbohydrates: 2G | Fiber: 1 g | Protein: 2 g

113.   Heavenly Keto Caramels

Servings: 6
Prep time: 15 minutes + 3-4 hours chill time

Ingredients:
1 c of butter
2 c of heavy whip cream
6 tbsp of stevia powder extract

Instructions:
1. Take a non-stick saucepan and place it over medium-low heat
2. Add butter and let it melt, heat until light brown
3. Add cream and stevia to butter and paddle for 2 minutes until sticky
4. Remove from heat and keep mixing
5. Pour into candy molds and chill for 3-4 hours
6. Serve and enjoy!

Nutritional Value per serving:
Calories: 242 | Fat: 44g | Carbohydrates: 1G | Net Carbohydrates: 0.5g | Fiber: 1 g | Protein: 1 g

114.   Chocolaty Crunchy Bars

Servings: 6
Prep time: 15 minutes + 2-3 hours chill time

Ingredients:
1 and ½ c of sugar-free chocolate chips
1 c of almond butter
Stevia to taste
¼ c of coconut oil
3 c of pecans, chopped

Instructions:
1. Take an 8-inch baking pan and layer with parchment paper
2. Take a bowl and mix in chips, butter, coconut oil, sweetener and mix well
3. Melt the mixture in the microwave for 2-3 minutes
4. Stir in nuts, seeds and mix well
5. Pour the batter into baking pan and spread evenly
6. Chill for 2-3 hours
7. Slice into small bars and enjoy!

Nutritional Value per serving:
Calories: 316 | Fat: 30g | Carbohydrates: 7g | Net Carbohydrates: 4g | Fiber: 1 g | Protein: 7 g

115.   Pinky Yogurt Popsicles

Servings: 6
Prep time: 15 minutes + 3-5 hours chill time

Ingredients:

8 oz frozen mango, diced
8 oz frozen strawberries
1 c of Greek yogurt
2 and ½ tsp of heavy whip cream
1 tsp of vanilla essence

Instructions:
1. Add the listed ingredients to your food processor and blend until smooth
2. Pour the mixture into popsicle molds
3. Freeze for 3-5 hours
4. Serve and enjoy!

Nutritional Value per serving:
Calories: 197 | Fat: 20G | Carbohydrates: 8g | Net Carbohydrates: 3g | Fiber: 2 g | Protein: 4 g

116.   Everybody's Favorite White Chocolate Bar

Servings: 6
Prep time: 15 minutes + 2-3 hours chill time

Ingredients:
2 and ½ oz cocoa butter
3 tbsp of swerving
1 tbsp of coconut milk powder
1 tsp of sunflower lecithin
1/8 tsp of stevia
1/8 tsp of monk fruit powder
½ tsp of vanilla extract

Instructions:
1. Take a pan and place it over medium heat, bring water to a boil and add coconut milk, cocoa butter, swerve, lecithin, stevia, and monk fruit
2. Wait until everything is mixed well
3. Remove the pan from heat and add vanilla
4. Pour batter into molds and let it chill for 2-3 hours
5. Remove from molds and enjoy!

Nutritional Value per serving:
Calories: 123 | Fat: 8g | Carbohydrates: 2G | Net Carbohydrates: 0.6g | Fiber: 1 g | Protein: 0 g

117.   Feisty Lemon Cheesecake Mousse

Servings: 5
Prep time: 10 minutes + 1 hour chill time

Ingredients:
8 oz mascarpone cheese
¼ c of fresh lemon juice
1 c of heavy cream
½ -1 tsp of liquid stevia
1/8 tsp of salt

Instructions:
1. Take a bowl and mix lemon and cream cheese using a mixer until the batter is smooth
2. Once the mixture is read, add heavy whip cream, salt, and stevia
3. Add more stevia if you want
4. Transfer the prepared crème to piping bag and pipe into serving glasses
5. Garnish with lemon zest and transfer to the fridge
6. Enjoy chilled!

Nutritional Value per serving:
Calories: 277 | Fat: 29g | Carbohydrates: 2G | Net Carbohydrates: 1.7g | Fiber: 0 g | Protein: 3.7 g

118.   No Bake Coconut Crack Bars
This is an easy recipe that is sure to satisfy your taste buds.
Serves: 22 bars
Prep: 1 min
Cook: 5 min
Ingredients:

Shredded and unsweetened coconut flakes - 3 cups

Maple syrup - 1/4 cup

Melted coconut oil - 1 cup

Chocolate chips - 1-2 cups
Directions:
1. Line an 8 by 10 loaf pan with a parchment paper.
2. Set aside.
3. Mix all the ingredients in a mixing bowl and pour the batter into the pan.
4. Wet your hand lightly and firmly press the batter into place.
5. Put in the freezer or refrigerator to make it firm.
6. Remove once firm and cut into bars.
7. Place the bars in the refrigerator.
8. Melt the chocolate chips and dip each bar until well coated.
9. Then place in the fridge until to firm the chocolate.
10. Serve.

Nutritional Info (Per Serving):
Calories 106, Fat 11g, Carbs 3g, Fiber 2g, Proteins 2g

119.   Keto Peanut Butter Fudge
Healthy, creamy and rich peanut butter fudge that is ready in minutes.
Serves: 18 cups
Prep: 2 min
Cook: 2 min
Ingredients:
Peanut butter - 1/2 cup
Liquid stevia – to taste
Coconut oil - 1/2 cup
Directions:
1. Line a muffin tin with liners and set aside.
2. Melt combined peanut butter and coconut oil on a stove-top.
3. Add in the stevia to the taste of your choice.

4. Divide above mixture into the muffin tins and freeze until it is firm.
5. Top with melted chocolate.
6. Enjoy.

Nutritional info (per serving):
Calories 89, Fat 8g, Carbs 1g, Fiber 1g, Protein 2g

120. Nutty Chocolate Delight

Servings: 6
Prep time: 10 minutes + 1 hour chill time

Ingredients:
2 and ½ oz of tahini butter
2 oz of almond butter
2 tbsp of Erythritol
Pinch of salt
½ tsp of vanilla extract
4 oz of melted cacao butter

Instructions:
1. Add tahini, almond butter to a blender alongside stevia and Erythritol and blend on low for 10 seconds
2. Add melted cacao butter slowly
3. Once the whole mix is added, blend for 15 seconds more
4. Pour into silicone molds and let it chill
5. Serve and enjoy!

Nutritional Value per serving:
Calories: 146 | Fat: 15G | Carbohydrates: 3g | Net Carbohydrates: 1.5G | Fiber: 1 g | Protein: 2 g

121. Healthy Vegan Protein Balls

Servings: 6
Prep time: 20 minutes + chill time

Ingredients:
1 c of creamed coconut
2 scoops Vegan Sports Chocolate Protein
¼ c of ground flax seed
½ tsp of vanilla extract
½ tsp of mint extract
1-2 tbsp of cocoa powder

Instructions:
1. Take a large sized bowl and melt the creamed coconut
2. Add the vanilla extract and stir well
3. Stir in flax seed, protein powder and knead until a fine dough forms
4. Form 24 balls and allow the balls to chill for 10-15 minutes
5. Roll them up in some cocoa powder if you prefer and serve!

Nutritional Value per serving:

Calories: 260 | Fat: 20G | Carbohydrates: 3g | Net Carbohydrates: 1G | Fiber: 1G | Protein: 10G

122. Easy Coconut Crack Bars

Servings: 6
Prep time: 5 minutes + 2-3 hours chill time

Ingredients:
3 c of shredded, unsweetened coconut flakes
¼ c of sugar-free maple syrup
1 c of melted coconut oil
1 -2 c of chocolate chips

Instructions:
1. Take an 8 x 10-inch loaf pan and line with parchment paper
2. Keep it on the side
3. Take a bowl and add all of the listed ingredients and pour the batter into your pan
4. Wet your hands lightly and firmly press the batter onto your pan
5. Transfer to fridge and let it chill
6. Once, slice into bars
7. Melt chocolate chips and dip each bar in chocolate
8. Let the coated bars chill and serve
9. Enjoy!

Nutritional Value per serving:
Calories: 106 | Fat: 11G | Carbohydrates: 3g | Net Carbohydrates: 2G | Fiber: 2g | Protein: 2G

123. Keto-Friendly Peanut Butter Fudge

Servings: 4
Prep time: 5 minutes + 2-3 hours chill time

Ingredients:
½ c of peanut butter
Liquid stevia to taste
½ c of coconut oil

Instructions:
1. Line your muffin tray with liners and keep them on the side
2. Melt peanut butter and coconut oil on the stove top and add stevia to your taste
3. Divide the mixture into your muffin tins and let it chill
4. Top with melted chocolate
5. Enjoy!

Nutritional Value per serving:
Calories: 89 | Fat: 8g | Carbohydrates: 1G | Net Carbohydrates: 0.5g | Fiber: 1G | Protein: 2G

124. Avocado And Lime Popsicle

Servings: 6
Prep time: 10 minutes + 7-8 hours

Ingredients:
2 avocados
1 and ½ c of coconut milk
¼ to Erythritol
2 tbsp of lime juice

Instructions:
1. Blend the listed ingredients in a blender until creamy
2. Distribute the blended mix into 6 popsicle molds and tap any air bubbles out
3. Place them in fridge and chill for 7-8 hours
4. Run water through molds and dislodge them
5. Enjoy!

Nutritional Value per serving:
Calories: 220 | Fat: 21G | Carbohydrates: 4.5g | Net Carbohydrates: 3.5g | Fiber: 1G | Protein: 2.5g

125. Keto Chia Pudding
Servings: 4
Nutritional Value per serving:: 12 g Net Carbs | 5 g Prot. | 24 g Fat | 273 Cal.

Ingredients:

- Whole ripe avocado – 1
- Chia seeds – .25 cup
- Medium dates – 2
- Almond or coconut milk – 1 cup
- Vanilla extract – .5 tsp.

Directions:

1. Pour the milk, vanilla, avocado, and dates into a blender.
2. Blend until well mixed. Empty over the chia seeds and cover overnight in the refrigerator when you go to bed. You can also let it rest for two to four hours before serving.

126. Lemon Custard – Slow Cooker

Servings: 4
Nutritional Value per serving:: 3 g Net Carbs | 7 g Prot. | 30 g Fat | 319 Cal.

Ingredients:

- Fresh lemon juice – .25 cup
- Large egg yolks – 5
- Lemon zest – 1 tbsp.
- Liquid stevia – .5 tsp.
- Vanilla extract – 1 tsp.
- Coconut cream/whipping cream – 2 cups
- Optional: Whipped coconut cream
- Also Needed: Ramekins/4 small jars

Directions:

1. Whisk the liquid stevia, egg yolks, lemon juice, lemon zest, and vanilla. Whip in the heavy cream. Divide into the four jars.
2. Add a rack in the cooker and arrange the jars on top of it. Add water to fill half of the way up the sides of the ramekins.
3. Secure the lid and cook three hours on low.
4. Transfer the jars from the cooker and cool to room temperature. Chill in the fridge approximately three hours.
5. Serve with the whipped cream if desired.

127.   Pumpkin Custard – Crockpot

Servings: 6
Nutritional Value per serving:: 3 g Net Carbs | 5 g Prot. | 12 g Fat | 147 Cal.

Ingredients:

- Large eggs – 4
- Granulated stevia/Erythritol blend – .5 cup
- Sea salt – .125 tsp.
- Vanilla extract – 1 tsp.
- Pumpkin pie spice – 1 tsp.
- Butter/coconut oil/ghee – 4 tbsp.
- Pumpkin puree Canned or homemade – 1 tsp.
- Super-fine almond flour – .5 cup
- Recommended Size for the Cooker: 3-4-quarts
- Coconut cooking oil spray or butter for the pot

Directions:

1. Take the butter out of the refrigerator to become room temperature. Lightly grease or spray the cooker.
2. Use a mixer to whisk the eggs – blending until smooth. Slowly, add the sweetener.
3. Blend in the vanilla extract and puree. Fold in the pie spice, salt, and almond flour. Mix everything well and add to the crockpot.
4. Secure the lid – with a paper towel between the top and the fixings to absorb moisture on top of the custard.
5. Cook for 2 to 2.75 hours on the low setting. When it's done, it will begin to pull away from the slow cooker. The center will be set.
6. Enjoy warm and top it off with garnishes as desired.

Candy

128.   Chocolate Bonbons

Servings: 6
Nutritional Value per serving:: -0- g Net Carbs | 1 g Prot. | 10 g Fat | 100 Cal.

Ingredients:

- Butter – 5 tbsp.

- Coconut oil – 3 tbsp.
- Sugar-free raspberry syrup – 2 tbsp.
- Cocoa powder – 2 tbsp.

Directions:

1. Mix the entire batch of ingredients in a pan.
2. Empty the bombs into six molds or muffin tins.
3. Place the prepared tin into the freezer for a minimum of two hours. Enjoy!

129.   Chocolate Coconut Bites

Servings: 6
Nutritional Value per serving:: 9 g Net Carbs | 9 g Prot. | 27 g Fat | 326 Cal.

Ingredients:

- Unsweetened 80% or higher dark chocolate – 4 oz.
- Heavy cream – .33 cup
- Coconut flour – 1 cup
- Chocolate protein powder – 1 tbsp.
- Shredded unsweetened coconut – .25 cup
- Coconut oil – 4 tbsp.

Directions:

1. Dice the dark chocolate into bits.
2. Warm up the heavy cream in a saucepan (med-low). Stir in the chocolate bits and oil. Continue stirring until combined and remove from the burner.
3. Stir in the protein powder and coconut flour. Store in the refrigerator for a minimum of two hours.
4. Take the dough out of the fridge when they are cool. Shape into balls and roll through the shredded coconut until coated.
5. Store in the fridge in a closed container.

130.   Chocolate Covered Almonds

Servings: 1
Nutritional Value per serving:: 3 g Net Carbs | 4 g Prot. | 15 g Fat | 183 Cal.

Ingredients:

- Unsweetened dark chocolate baking chips – .75 cup
- Whole raw almonds – 1.5 cups
- Pure vanilla extract – 1 tsp.
- Sea salt – 1 pinch

Directions:

1. Cut a piece of parchment paper and cover a baking tray.
2. Toss the chips into a saucepan using low heat. Stir and add the vanilla.
3. Once the chocolate is melted, add the almonds and stir until coated.

4. Arrange them on the baking tin and dust with the salt.
5. Place in the fridge for a minimum of 30 minutes before you are ready to devour your portion.
6. For a taste change, sprinkle with some ground cinnamon.

131.   Coconut Peanut Butter Balls
Servings: 15
Nutritional Value per serving:: 0.92 g Net Carbs | 0.98 g Prot. | 3.19 g Fat | 35.1 Cal.

Ingredients:

- Creamy peanut butter – Keto-friendly – 3 tbsp.
- Powdered Erythritol – 2.5 tsp.
- Unsweetened cocoa powder – 3 tsp.
- Almond flour – 2 tsp.
- Unsweetened coconut flakes – .5 cup

Directions:

1. Combine the peanut butter, Erythritol, cocoa, and flour. Place in the freezer for one hour.
2. Spoon out a small spoon size of the butter mix. Roll into the flakes until it is covered.
3. Refrigerate overnight for the best results and enjoy.

132.   Cream Cheese Truffles – Party Time
Servings: 24
Nutritional Value per serving:: 1.67 g Net Carbs | 1.23 g Prot. | 7 g Fat | 72.7 Cal.

Ingredients:
- Cream cheese, softened – 16 oz.
- Unsweetened cocoa powder – divided – .5 cup
- Swerve confectioners – 4 tbsp.
- Liquid Stevia – .25 tsp.
- Rum extract – .5 tsp.
- Instant coffee – 1 tbsp.
- Water – 2 tbsp.
- Heavy whipping cream – 1 tbsp.
- Paper candy cups for serving – 24

Directions:

1. Combine all of the fixings (set aside 1/4 cup of cocoa powder). Blend well with a hand mixer. Chill in the fridge for about 30 minutes.
2. Dust the countertop with the rest of the cocoa powder. Roll out heaping tablespoons of the mixture in your hands to form about 24 balls.
3. Roll the balls through the powder and place into individual candy cups.
4. Chill for another hour before serving.

133.   Crust-less Cheesecake Bites
Servings: 4
Nutritional Value per serving:: 2 g Net Carbs | 5 g Prot. | 15 g Fat | 169 Cal.

Ingredients:

- **Large eggs – 2**
- **Sour cream – .25 cup**
- **Vanilla extract – .25 tsp.**
- **Room temperature cream cheese – 4 oz.**
- **Natural sweetener – ex. swerve – .33 cup**

Directions:

1. Warm up the oven to reach 350°F. Use a hand mixer to combine the ingredients.
2. Prepare a cupcake pan with 4 disposable paper cups or silicone liners.
3. Fill the cups and bake for 30 minutes.
4. After cooling about 3 hours, serve and enjoy.
5. You can save the extras for up to 3 months if stored in zip-lock type bags.

134. Coconut Macaroons Fat Bombs

Servings: 10
Nutritional Value per serving:: 0.5 g Net Carbs | 1.8 g Prot. | 5 g Fat | 46 Cal.

Ingredients:

- Shredded coconut – .5 cup
- Organic almond flour – .25 cup
- Swerve – 2 tbsp.
- Coconut oil – 1 tbsp.
- Vanilla extract – 1 tbsp.
- Egg whites – 3

Directions:

1. In a mixing bowl, blend the swerve, coconut, and almond flour until well combined.
2. Warm the oil in a saucepan and stir in the vanilla.
3. Place a medium-sized bowl in the freezer.
4. Combine the oil into the flour mixture, mixing well.
5. Put the whites of the eggs into the cold dish and whisk until stiff – foamy peaks are formed. Fold in the whites with the flour.
6. Scoop the mixture into the baking sheet/muffin cups.
7. Bake until the macaroons are lightly browned or about eight minutes.
8. Cool before placing on a serving dish.

135. Coffee Fat Bombs

Servings: 15
Nutritional Value per serving:: -0- g Net Carbs | 4 g Fat | -0- g Prot. | 45 Cal.

Ingredients:

- Cream cheese – room temperature – 4.4 oz.
- Powdered Xylitol – 2 tbsp.
- Instant coffee – 1 tbsp.
- Coconut oil – 1 tbsp.
- Unsweetened cocoa powder – 1 tbsp.

- Room temperature butter – 1 tbsp.

Instructions:

1. Take the butter and cream cheese out of the fridge about an hour before it's time to begin.
2. With a blender/food processor, blitz the xylitol and coffee into a fine powder. Add the hot water to form a pasty mix.
3. Blend in the butter, cream cheese, cocoa powder, and coconut oil.
4. Add to ice cube trays and freeze a minimum of one to two hours.
5. Use Ziploc bags to keep them fresh in the freezer.

136.   Coffee Fat Bombs

Servings: 15
Nutritional Value per serving:: -0- g Net Carbs | -0- g Prot. | 4 g Fat | 45 Cal.

Ingredients:

- Cream cheese – room temperature – 4.4 oz.
- Powdered xylitol – 2 tbsp.
- Instant coffee – 1 tbsp.
- Room temperature butter – 1 tbsp.
- Coconut oil – 1 tbsp.
- Unsweetened cocoa powder – 1 tbsp.

Directions:

1. With a blender/food processor, blitz the xylitol and coffee into a fine powder. Add the hot water to form a pasty mix.
2. Blend in the butter, cream cheese, cocoa powder, and coconut oil.
3. Add to ice cube trays and freeze a minimum of one to two hours.
4. Use Ziploc bags to keep them fresh in the freezer.

137.   Craving Buster Fat Bombs

Servings: 32
Nutritional Value per serving:: 2.25 g Net Carbs | 1.75 g Prot. | 22.5 g Fat | 122.5 Cal.

Ingredients:

- Organic cacao powder – 1 cup
- Melted organic coconut oil – 1 cup
- Almond butter – 1 cup
- Muffin tins – 32-count

Directions:

1. Melt the oil and whisk in with the almond butter and cacao.
2. Spoon 1/2 tablespoon of the product into the 32 small paper muffin cups.
3. Freeze or refrigerate until hard and store in the fridge.
4. Note: If you want just one bomb; melt the oil and just add 1/2 tablespoon of each ingredient to enjoy.

138. Dark Chocolate Fat Bombs

Servings: 12
Nutritional Value per serving:: 5.6 g Net Carbs | 10.5 g Fat | 4 g Prot. | 96 Cal.

Ingredients:

- Stevia extract – 1 tsp.
- Butter/coconut oil – .5 cup
- Almond butter – .5 cup
- Dark chocolate – 85% or higher – 3 oz.
- **Sea salt – .25 tsp.**

Directions:

1. With the use of a double boiler, combine all of the components in the recipe until smooth.
2. Empty the mixture into 12 ice trays and freeze for a minimum of one hour.
3. Serve or enjoy when the sugar urge strikes.

139. Dark Chocolate Raspberry Fat Bombs

Servings: 14
Nutritional Value per serving:: 2.6 g Net Carbs | 2.2 g Prot. | 17 g Fat | 164 Cal.

Ingredients:

- Extra-virgin coconut oil – 3 tbsp.
- Cocoa butter – .5 cup
- Unsweetened dark chocolate – 100% cacao – 4.2 oz.
- Unsweetened vanilla extract – 1 tsp. or 1 vanilla bean
- Unsweetened cacao powder – .33 cup
- Stevia extract – vanilla/clear/chocolate – 20-25 drops
- Swerve or Erythritol – powdered – 1/2 – 3/4 cup

Directions:

1. Roast the almonds in a pan for five minutes.
2. Add an almond to each raspberry and freeze for one hour.
3. Using a dish over a pan of hot water or a double boiler, melt the unsweetened chocolate, coconut oil, and cocoa butter. Powder the Swerve for a smooth texture in a blender.
4. Remove the seeds from the bean (if using) by slicing the bean lengthwise and scraping out the seeds. Add them along with the unsweetened cacao, stevia, and powdered Erythritol.
5. Pour the mixture into papers with the use of a mini muffin tin, one tablespoon for each one. Add two loaded raspberries and pour one more tablespoon of the chocolate to cover.
6. Put the bombs in the freezer until set, for about 30 minutes.

140. Lemonade Fat Bombs

Servings: 2
Nutritional Value per serving:: 7 g Net Carbs | 4 g Prot. | 43 g Fat | 404 Cal.

Ingredients:

- **Cream cheese – 4 oz.**

- **Butter – 2 oz.**
- **Lemon zest & juice – .5 of 1 lemon**
- **Swerve – 2 tsp.**
- **Pink Himalayan salt – 1 pinch or to taste**

Directions:

1. **Take the butter and cream cheese out of the fridge and let it become room temperature before using. Zest the lemon and juice it into a small dish.**
2. **In another container, mix the butter with the cream cheese. Use a hand mixer to combine all of the fixings until well mixed.**
3. **Spoon the mixture into small molds or cupcake paper liners in a muffin tin pan.**
4. **Stick the chosen holder in the freezer for two hours. Take them out of the molds and put them in a zipper-top baggie to enjoy any time. Store in the freezer for up to three months.**

141.   Maple Almond Fudge Fat Bombs
Servings: 24
Nutritional Value per serving:: 1.5 g Net Carbs | 1 g Prot. | 6 g Fat | 58 Cal.

Ingredients:

- Coconut oil – 2 tbsp.
- Butter – .25 cup
- All-natural almond butter – .5 cup
- Sugar-free maple syrup – 1 tbsp.
- Also Needed: Mini muffin tin & paper liners

Directions:

1. Melt the butter, almond butter, and coconut oil for two minutes in the microwave. Stir every 30 seconds until melted. Whisk in the syrup and stir.
2. Pour the fixings into the prepared tins. Place in the fridge until hardened. Dice into 24 bite-sized pieces.
3. You can also store in the freezer or at room temperature, depending on the desired consistency.

142.   Pistachio & Almond Fat Bombs
Servings: 36
Nutritional Value per serving:: 3.1 g Net Carbs | 2.2 g Prot. | 17.4 g Fat | 170 Cal.

Ingredients:

- Roasted almond butter – 1 cup
- Firm coconut oil – 1 cup
- Creamy coconut butter – 1 cup
- Cacao butter – melted – .5 cup
- Full-fat coconut milk – .5 cup
- Chai spice – 2 tsp.
- Ghee – .25 cup
- Pure vanilla extract – 1 tbsp.
- Raw shelled pistachios – .25 tsp.

- Himalayan salt – .25 tsp.
- Pure almond extract – .25 tsp.
- Also Needed: 9-inch square baking pan

Directions:

1. Chill the coconut milk overnight.
2. Grease the pan and line it with parchment paper.
3. Melt the butter in a saucepan or microwave and set aside.
4. Add everything except the pistachios and cacao butter in a large bowl. Use the slow speeds and increase using a hand mixer until it is airy and light.
5. Empty the melted cacao into the almond mix and continue mixing until it is well incorporated.
6. Add it to the prepared pan and sprinkle with the chopped pistachios.
7. Refrigerate at least four hours. It is much better if chilled overnight.
8. Cut into 36 squares and enjoy.

143.   Raspberry Coconut Bark Fat Bombs
Servings: 12
Nutritional Value per serving:: 2.45 g Net Carbs | 1.7 g Prot. | 23.6 g Fat | 234 Cal.

Ingredients:

- Powdered swerve sweetener – .25 cup
- Freeze-dried raspberries – .5 cup
- Coconut oil – .5 cup
- Coconut butter – .5 cup
- Unsweetened shredded coconut – .5 cup
- Also Needed: 8 x 8 pan with parchment paper

Directions:

1. Prepare the baking pan and grind the berries in a food processor or coffee grinder until they are powdery.
2. Using the medium heat setting, add the oil, butter, sweetener, and coconut in a small saucepan. Stir until combined.
3. Pour half of the mixture into the pan and add the raspberry mixture to the other half of the batter and stir.
4. Drop by the spoonful into the coconut base and swirl to make a pretty design. Refrigerate or freeze and break into chunks for a tasty snack.

144.   Stuffed Pecan Fat Bombs
Servings: 1
Nutritional Value per serving:: 2 g Net Carbs | 11 g Prot. | 31 g Fat | 150 Cal.

Ingredients:

- Pecan halves – 4
- Neufchatel cheese/cream cheese – 1 oz.
- Coconut butter/unsalted butter – .5 tbsp.
- Sea salt – 1 pinch

- Your favorite flavor mix – herb or veggie

Directions:

1. Warm up the oven to 350°F oven. Once it's hot, toast the pecans for 8 to 10 minutes. Let cool.
2. Allow the cream cheese and butter to soften. Add the mixture with your favorite flavor, veggie, or herb and mix until smooth.
3. Spread the tasty fixings between the two pecan halves.
4. Drizzle with some sea salt.

145. Banana Split Cheesecake – No-Bake

Servings: 20
Nutritional Value per serving:: 6.7 g Net Carbs | 4.1 g Prot. | 30 g Fat | 302 Cal.

Ingredients for the Crust:
- Cinnamon – 2 tsp.
- Almond flour – 3 cups
- Swerve – .33 cup
- Melted butter – 1 cup

Ingredients for the Filling:
- Swerve confectioner's sugar – 1 cup
- Melted butter – 1 cup
- Cream cheese – 16 oz.

Ingredients for the Topping:
- Chopped banana – 1
- Sliced strawberries – 2 pints
- Lemon juice – 1 tbsp.
- Heavy whipping cream – 2 cups
- Gelatin – 1.5 tsp.
- Vanilla extract – 1 tsp.
- Swerve – 3 tbsp.
- Nuts – optional
- Water – 3 tbsp.
- Chocolate sauce – optional
- Also Needed: 9 x 13-inch pan

Directions:
1. Combine the crust fixings and press together in the pan.
2. Mix the sweetener, melted butter, and cream cheese until creamy. Spread on top of the crust.
3. Combine the banana and strawberries in a mixing dish along with the lemon juice. Make the next layer.
4. Prepare the Topping: Combine the whipping cream and gelatin in the water and beat well. Blend in the vanilla extract and sweetener. Whip until it is creamy to cover and make the next layer.
5. Top with the chocolate sauce and nuts if you like it that way.

146. Cheesecake Cupcakes

Servings: 12
Nutritional Value per serving:: 2.1 g Net Carbs | 4.9 g Prot. | 20 g Fat | 204 Cal.

Ingredients:

- Butter – .25 cup – melted
- Almond meal – .5 cup
- Eggs – 2
- Softened cream cheese – 16 oz. pkg.
- Stevia or your favorite sweetener – .75 cup
- Vanilla extract – 1 tsp.

Directions:

1. Warm up the oven until it reaches 350°F. Prepare a muffin tin with 12 paper liners.
2. Combine the butter and almond meal. Spoon into the cups to make a flat crust.
3. Whisk the vanilla, sweetener of choice, eggs, and cream cheese with an electric mixer until creamy. Scoop it in on top of the crust. Bake for 15-17 minutes.
4. Once they're done the cooking cycle, just remove and cool at room temperature. Store overnight or at least 8 hours.
5. Enjoy anytime for a delicious treat.

147. Individual Strawberry Cheesecakes
Servings: 4
Nutritional Value per serving:: 9 g Net Carbs | 8 g Prot. | 47 g Fat | 489 Cal.

Ingredients for the Crust:

- Almond flour – .5 cup
- Melted butter/coconut oil – 3 tbsp.
- Sugar substitute – your preference – .25 cup or Maple syrup

Ingredients for the Filling:

- Sugar substitute – 3 tbsp. or use Grade B maple syrup
- Strawberries – 6
- Cream cheese – 8 oz.
- Sour cream – .33 cup
- Pure vanilla extract – .5 tsp.

Ingredients for the Garnish:

- Strawberries – 4
- Fresh mint leaves

Directions:

1. Combine the crust fixings in a mixing bowl. Blend well and divide into four small ramekins. Gently press with your fingers.
2. Prepare the filling in a food processor. Pulse until creamy smooth.
3. Divide it over the crust of each one and chill for an hour or until it's set.
4. Garnish with another berry if desired and serve. (Add the carbs for any added garnishes)

148. Lemon Mousse Cheesecake
Servings: 1
Nutritional Value per serving:: 1.7 g Net Carbs | 3.7 g Prot. | 30 g Fat | 277 Cal.

Ingredients:

- Lemon juice – 2 lemons approx. – .25 cup
- Cream cheese – 8 oz.
- Salt – .125 tsp.
- Lemon liquid Stevia – 1 tsp. or to your liking
- Heavy cream – 1 cup
Directions:

1. Use a mixer to blend the lemon juice and cream cheese until it's creamy smooth. Add the remainder of the ingredients and whip until blended.
2. Taste test. Add to a serving dish and sprinkle with some lemon zest.
3. Refrigerate until you are ready to enjoy.

149.   New York Cheesecake Cupcakes

Servings: 12
Nutritional Value per serving:: 14.7 g Net Carbs | 6.5g Prot. | 26.7 g Fat | 273 Cal.

Ingredients:

- Melted butter – 5 tbsp.
- Almond meal – .66 cup
- Cream cheese – 16 oz.
- Sour cream – .5 cup
- Swerve or another favorite – .75 cup
- Water – 2 tbsp.
- Heavy whipping cream – .25 cup
- Eggs -3
- Almond flour – 2 tbsp.
- Vanilla extract – 1.5 tsp.

Directions:

1. Heat up the oven to reach 350°F. Prepare a 12-count muffin pan with paper liners.
2. Combine the butter and almond meal and spoon into the liners to form the crust.
3. Stir the sweetener and cream cheese until creamy. Blend in with the water and whipping cream. One at a time, add the eggs, stirring with each one.
4. Next, fold in the flour, sour cream, and extract. Spoon into the liners.
5. Bake for 15-18 minutes. Don't over-cook. The middle will be set when it's done. Cool on the countertop until room temperature. Then, store in the fridge **overnight or a minimum of 8 hours.**

150.   Plain Cheesecake – No Bake

Servings: 6
Nutritional Value per serving:: 5 g Net Carbs | 6.9 g Prot. | 25 g Fat | 247 Cal.

Ingredients for the Crust:

- Melted coconut oil – 2 tbsp.
- Almond flour – 2 tbsp.
- Swerve Confectioner's/equivalent – 2 tbsp.

- Crushed salted almonds – 2 tbsp.

Filling Ingredients:

- Swerve confectioner's/equivalent – .25 cup
- Gelatin – 1 tsp.
- Cream cheese – 16 oz. pkg.
- Unsweetened almond milk – .5 cup
- Vanilla extract – 1 tsp.

Directions:

1. Prepare the crust by combining all of the fixings under the crust section. Place one heaping tablespoon into the bottom of dessert cups. Press the mixture down and set aside.
2. Prepare the filling. Mix the sweetener and gelatin. Pour in the milk and stir (5 min.). Whip the vanilla beans and cream cheese with a mixer on medium until creamy. Add the gelatin mixture slowly until well incorporated.
3. Pour the mixture over the crust of each cup. Chill for three hours, minimum.

151. Chocolate & Mint Smoothie
Servings: 1
Nutritional Value per serving:: 6.5 g Net Carbs | 5 g Prot. | 40 g Fat | 401 Cal.

Directions:

Ingredients:

- Medium avocado – .5 of 1
- Coconut milk – .25 cup
- Unsweetened cashew/almond milk – 1 cup
- Swerve/Erythritol – 2 tbsp.
- Cocoa powder – 1 tbsp.
- Fresh mint leaves – 3-4
- MCT oil – 1 tbsp.
- Ice cubes – 2-3
- Optional: Coconut milk or whipped cream

Directions:

1. Mix all of the ingredients in your blender.
2. Add ice cubes, as many as you like. Add the topping if preferred.
3. Serve and enjoy!

152. Chocolate Smoothie
Servings: 1 large
Nutritional Value per serving:: 4.4 g Net Carbs | 34.5 g Prot. | 46 g Fat | 570 Cal.

Ingredients:

- Large eggs – 2
- Almond or coconut butter – 1-2 tbsp.

- Extra-virgin coconut oil – 1 tbsp.
- Coconut milk or heavy whipping cream – .25 cup
- Chia seeds – 1-2 tbsp.
- Cinnamon – .5 tsp.
- Plain or chocolate whey protein – .25 cup
- Stevia extract – 3-5 drops
- Unsweetened cacao powder – 1 tbsp.
- Water – .25 cup
- Ice – .5 cup
- Vanilla extract – .5 tsp.

Directions:

1. Add the eggs along with the rest of fixings into the blender.
2. Pulse until frothy. Add to a chilled glass and enjoy.

153. Cinnamon Roll Smoothie
Servings: 1
Nutritional Value per serving:: 0.6 g Net Carbs | 26.5 g Prot. | 3.25 g Fat | 145 Cal.
Ingredients:
- Almond milk – 1 cup
- Vanilla protein powder – 2 tbsp.
- Vanilla extract – .25 tsp.
- Cinnamon – .5 tsp.
- Sweetener – 4 tsp.
- Flax meal – 1 tsp.
- Ice – 1 cup
Directions:
1. Combine all of the fixings in a blender. Add the ice last.
2. Blend on the high setting for 30 seconds until thickened.

154. 5-Minute Mocha Smoothie
Servings: 3
Nutritional Value per serving:: 4 g Net Carbs | 3 g Prot. | 16 g Fat | 176 Cal.
Ingredients:
- Unsweetened almond milk – 1.5 cups
- Coconut milk – from the can – .5 cup
- Vanilla extract – 1 tsp.
- Instant coffee crystals – regular or decaffeinated – 1 tsp.
- Erythritol blend/granulated stevia- 3 tbsp.
- Unsweetened cocoa powder – 3 tbsp.
- Avocado – 1
Directions:
1. Use a sharp knife to slice the avocado in half. Scoop the center out and discard the pit. Dice the avocado and add it along with the rest of the ingredients into the blender.
2. Mix well until smooth and serve.

155. Raspberry Avocado Smoothie
Servings: 2
Nutritional Value per serving:: 4 g Net Carbs | 2.5 g Prot. | 20 g Fat | 227 Cal.

Ingredients:

- Ripe avocado – 1
- Lemon juice – 3 tbsp.
- Water – 1.33 cups
- Frozen unsweetened raspberries/or choice of berries – .5 cup
- Your preference sugar equivalent – 1 tbsp. (+) 1 t.

Directions:

1. *Blend all of the components in a blender until creamy smooth.*
2. *Empty the smoothie into two chilled glasses and enjoy!*

156. Raspberry Chocolate Cheesecake Smoothie

Servings: 1

Nutritional Value per serving:: 7 g Net Carbs | 6.9 g Prot. | 54 g Fat | 512 Cal.

Ingredients:

- Frozen or fresh raspberries – .33 cup
- Coconut milk/heavy whipping cream – .25 cup
- Full-fat cream cheese/creamed coconut milk – .25 cup
- Unsweetened cacao powder – 1 tbsp.
- Extra-virgin coconut oil – 1 tbsp.
- Water – .5 cup
- Liquid stevia extract – 3-5 drops – optional

Directions:

1. Place all of the goodies for your smoothie in a blender.
2. Blend until frothy and smooth. Pour into a chilled glass and relax.

157. Strawberry Almond Smoothies

Servings: 2

Nutritional Value per serving:: 7 g Net Carbs | 15 g Prot. | 25 g Fat | 304 Cal.

Ingredients:

- Heavy cream – .5 cup
- Unsweetened almond milk – 16 oz.
- Stevia to taste
- Frozen unsweetened strawberries – .25 cup
- Whey vanilla isolate powder – 2 tbsp.

Directions:

1. Combine each of the fixings into a blender.
2. Puree until smooth. Add a small amount of water to thin the smoothie.

158. Vanilla Smoothie

Servings: 1

Nutritional Value per serving:: 4 g Net Carbs | 12 g Prot. | 64 g Fat | 651 Cal.

Ingredients:

- Mascarpone full-fat cheese – .5 cup
- Large egg yolks – 2
- Water – .25 cup
- Coconut oil – 1 tbsp.
- Ice cubes – 4
- Liquid stevia 3 drops
- Pure vanilla extract – .5 tsp.
- Optional Topping: Whipped cream

Directions:

1. Combine each of the ingredients in a blender until smooth.
2. Add the whipped cream for a special treat but add the carbs if any.

159.   Raspberry Cold Treat

Preparation time: 2 hours
Cooking time: 10 minutes
Servings: 4

Ingredients:

- 1 and ½ cups raspberries
- 2 cups water

Directions:

1. Put raspberries and water in a pan, bring to a boil over medium heat, simmer for 10 minutes, divide into small ramekins and keep in the freezer for 2 hours.
Enjoy!

Nutritional Value per serving: calories 60, fat 0, fiber 0, carbs 3, protein 2

160.   Cocoa and Peanut Brownies

Preparation time: 10 minutes
Cooking time: 30 minutes
Servings: 4

Ingredients:

- 1 egg
- 1/3 cup cocoa powder
- 1/3 cup stevia
- 7 tablespoons ghee, melted
- ½ teaspoon vanilla extract
- ¼ cup almond flour
- ¼ cup walnuts, chopped
- ½ teaspoon baking powder
- 1 tablespoon peanut butter

Directions:

1. Heat up a pan with 6 tablespoons ghee and the ghee over medium heat, stir, cook for 5 minutes, transfer to a bowl, add vanilla extract, cocoa powder, egg, baking powder, walnuts and almond flour, stir really well and pour into a skillet.

2. In a bowl, mix 1-tablespoon ghee with peanut butter, heat up in your microwave for a few seconds, stir, drizzle this over brownies mix, introduce in the oven at 350 degrees F, bake for 30 minutes, cut and serve.
Enjoy!

Nutritional Value per serving: calories 203, fat 32, fiber 1, carbs 3, protein 6

161.   Peach Pie

Preparation time: 10 minutes
Cooking time: 30 minutes
Servings: 4

Ingredients:
- 4 cups peaches, peeled and sliced
- ¼ cup coconut sugar
- ½ teaspoon cinnamon powder
- 1 and ½ cups coconut, shredded
- ¼ cup stevia
- ¼ teaspoon nutmeg, ground
- ½ cup almond milk
- 1 teaspoon vanilla extract
- Cooking spray

Directions:
1. In a bowl, mix peaches with coconut sugar, cinnamon, and stir.
2. In another bowl, mix the coconut with stevia, nutmeg, almond milk and vanilla extract and stir.
3. Spray a pie pan with cooking spray, spread peaches, add cinnamon mix on top, introduce in the oven and bake at 350 degrees F for 30 minutes.
4. Serve cold.
Enjoy!

Nutritional Value per serving: calories 202, fat 4, fiber 4, carbs 7, protein 3

162.   Plums and Cinnamon

Preparation time: 10 minutes
Cooking time: 20 minutes
Servings: 6

Ingredients:
- 1 pound plums, stoned and halved
- 1 and ¼ cups coconut sugar
- 1 teaspoon cinnamon powder
- ¼ cup water

Directions:
1. In a pan, combine the plums with sugar, cinnamon and water, stir, cover, boil over medium heat for 20 minutes, divide into cups and serve cold.
Enjoy!

Nutritional Value per serving: calories 150, fat 2, fiber 1, carbs 2, protein 3

163. Stewed Bananas

Preparation time: 10 minutes
Cooking time: 10 minutes
Servings: 4

Ingredients:
- Juice of ½ lemon
- 3 tablespoons apple juice, unsweetened
- 1 tablespoon coconut oil
- 4 bananas, peeled and sliced

Directions:
1. Arrange bananas in a pan, add the apple juice, lemon juice and oil, toss, cook over medium-high heat, cook for 10 minutes, divide into bowls and serve.
Enjoy!

Nutritional Value per serving: calories 120, fat 1, fiber 2, carbs 6, protein 3

164. Mascarpone and Berries

Preparation time: 10 minutes
Cooking time: 0 minutes
Servings: 4

Ingredients:
- 8 ounces mascarpone cheese
- 1 cup coconut cream
- 1 teaspoon stevia
- 1 pint berries

Directions:
1. In a bowl combine the mascarpone with stevia and coconut cream and whisk well.
2. Add berries, fold them gently, divide into cups and serve cold.
Enjoy!

Nutritional Value per serving: calories 165, fat 2, fiber 2, carbs 4, protein 2

165. Macadamia Custard

Preparation time: 10 minutes
Cooking time: 40 minutes
Servings: 4

Ingredients:
- 1 cup coconut milk
- 4 eggs
- 1/3 cup coconut cream
- 1/3 cup macadamia butter
- 1/3 cup stevia
- 1 teaspoon vanilla extract

Directions:

1. In a bowl, combine the coconut milk with the eggs, coconut cream, macadamia buttes, stevia and vanilla, whisk well and pour into 4 ramekins.
2. Put some water in a roasting pan, add ramekins, introduce in the oven and bake at 325 degrees F for 40 minutes.
3. Serve the custard cold.
   Enjoy!

Nutritional Value per serving: calories 263, fat 12, fiber 3, carbs 4, protein 6

166.   Coconut Raspberry Cake
Preparation time: 1 hour and 10 minutes
Cooking time: 10 minutes
Servings: 6

Ingredients:
For the biscuit:
- 2 cups almond flour
- 1 egg
- 1 tablespoon ghee, melted
- ½ teaspoon baking soda
  For the coconut layer:
- 1 cup coconut milk
- ¼ cup coconut oil, melted
- 3 cups coconut, shredded
- 1/3 cup stevia
- 1 teaspoon vanilla extract
  For the raspberry layer:
- 1 cup raspberries
- 1 teaspoon stevia
- 3 tablespoons chia seeds
- 2 tablespoons water

Directions:
1. In a bowl, combine the almond flour with the eggs, ghee and baking soda, stir well, press on the bottom of springform pan, introduce in the oven at 350 degrees F for 15 minutes and leave aside to cool down.
2. Meanwhile, in a pan, combine the raspberries with 1-teaspoon stevia, chia seeds and water, stir, cook for 5 minutes, take off heat, cool down and spread over the biscuit layer.
3. In another small pan, combine the coconut milk with the coconut, oil, 1/3 cup stevia and vanilla extract, stir for 1-2 minutes, take off heat, cool down and spread over the coconut milk.
4. Cool the cake in the fridge for 1 hour, slice and serve.
   Enjoy!

Nutritional Value per serving: calories 241, fat 12, fiber 4, carbs 5, protein 5

167.   Coconut Cookies
Preparation time: 10 minutes
Cooking time: 20 minutes
Servings: 6

Ingredients:
- 1 cup almond flour
- ½ cup cocoa chips
- ½ cup coconut flakes
- 1/3 cup stevia
- ½ cup almond butter
- ¼ cup ghee, melted
- 2 eggs

Directions:
1. In a bowl, combine the flour with the cocoa chips, coconut flakes and stevia and stir.
2. Add almond butter, ghee and eggs, whisk well, spoon medium cookies on a lined baking sheet, introduce in the oven and cook at 350 degrees F for 20 minutes.
3. Serve the cookies cold.
   Enjoy!

Nutritional Value per serving: calories 200, fat 12, fiber 4, carbs 3, protein 5

168.   Coconut Balls
Preparation time: 1 hour and 10 minutes
Cooking time: 0 minutes
Servings: 4

Ingredients:
- 3 tablespoons peanut butter, soft
- 3 teaspoons cocoa powder
- 2 and ½ teaspoons stevia
- 2 teaspoons almond flour
- ½ cup coconut, shredded

Directions:
1. In a bowl, mix the peanut butter with the cocoa powder, stevia and flour, stir well and keep in the freezer for 1 hour.
2. Spoon small amounts of cocoa mix into the coconut, dredge them and serve.
   Enjoy!

Nutritional Value per serving: calories 40, fat 2, fiber 3, carbs 3, protein 3

169.   Cream Cheese Candies
Preparation time: 1 hour
Cooking time: 0 minutes
Servings: 12

Ingredients:
- 16 ounces cream cheese
- ½ cup cocoa powder
- 3 tablespoons stevia
- ½ teaspoon vanilla extract
- 1 tablespoon instant coffee
- 2 tablespoons water
- 1 tablespoons coconut cream

Directions:

1. In a bowl, combine the cream cheese with cocoa powder, stevia, vanilla extract, coffee, water and cream, stir, divide into small candy cups and keep in the fridge for 1 hour.
Enjoy!

Nutritional Value per serving: calories 100, fat 4, fiber 4, carbs 3, protein 4

170. Blueberry, Dates and Banana Cream

Preparation time: 5 minutes
Cooking time: 0 minutes
Servings: 2

Ingredients:
- ¾ cup blueberries
- 1 tablespoon peanut butter
- ¾ cup almond milk
- ½ banana, peeled
- 2 dates

Directions:

1. In a blender, combine the blueberries with the milk, banana, butter and dates, pulse well, divide into 2 glasses and serve.
Enjoy!

Nutritional Value per serving: calories 120, fat 3, fiber 3, carbs 6, protein 11

171. Almond Cherry Cobbler

Preparation time: 10 minutes
Cooking time: 1 hour
Servings: 10

Ingredients:
- 1 cup almond FLOUR+1 tablespoon
- 1 cup coconut sugar
- ½ cup coconut butter, melted
- 1 teaspoon baking powder
- 2 cups cherries, pitted
- ¾ cup palm sugar
- 1 cup milk

Directions:

1. In a bowl, mix 1-cup flour with coconut sugar, baking powder and the milk and stir well.
2. Put the melted butter in a baking dish, add the coconut mix over it and do not stir.
3. In a bowl, mix the cherries with 1-tablespoon flour and palm sugar, toss, spread over the batter in the baking dish, introduce in the oven and cook at 350 degrees F for 1 hour.
4. Serve cold.
Enjoy!

Nutritional Value per serving: calories 190, fat 4, fiber 5, carbs 6, protein 10

172.   Apples and Raisins
Preparation time: 10 minutes
Cooking time: 20 minutes
Servings: 4

Ingredients:
- 4 big apples, cored, and tops cut off
- A handful raisins
- 1 tablespoon cinnamon powder

Directions:
1. Stuff each apple with raisins, sprinkle cinnamon, arrange in a baking dish and bake in the oven at 375 degrees F for 20 minutes.
   Enjoy!

Nutritional Value per serving: calories 200, fat 3, fiber 4, carbs 6, protein 10

173.   Pumpkin Brownies
Preparation time: 10 minutes
Cooking time: 15 minutes
Servings: 12

Ingredients:
- 2 and ½ cups almond flour
- ½ teaspoon baking soda
- 1 tablespoon flax seed
- 3 tablespoons water
- ½ cup pumpkin flesh, mashed
- 2 tablespoons coconut butter
- 1 teaspoon vanilla extract

Directions:
1. In a bowl, mix flax seed with water and stir.
2. In another bowl, mix flour with salt and baking soda.
3. In a third bowl, mix pumpkin puree with butter, vanilla extract and flaxseed.
4. Add the flour, stir, scoop tablespoons of brownie mix on a lined baking sheet, introduce them in the oven at 350 degrees F and bake for 15 minutes.
5. Serve them cold.
   Enjoy!

Nutritional Value per serving: calories 140, fat 2, fiber 2, carbs 7, protein 6

174.   Blueberry Lemon Curd
Preparation time: 10 minutes
Cooking time: 5 minutes
Servings: 4

Ingredients:
- 2 cups blueberries
- ¼ cup lemon juice

- 2/3 cup coconut sugar
- 2 teaspoons lemon zest, grated
- 4 tablespoons coconut butter, soft
- 3 egg yolks, whisked

Directions:
1. Heat up a small pan over medium heat, add blueberries and lemon juice, stir, bring to a simmer, strain into a bowl, mash, add sugar, lemon zest, butter and egg yolks, whisk well, transfer to the pan again, cook over medium-low heat and cook for 5 minutes.
2. Divide into cups and serve cold.
   Enjoy!

Nutritional Value per serving: calories 140, fat 3, fiber 3, carbs 6, protein 7

175. Cold Apricot and Avocado Cake
Preparation time: 4 hours and 5 minutes
Cooking time: 0 minutes
Servings: 4

Ingredients:
- 12 ounces apricots, chopped
- 2 tablespoons chia seeds
- 1 tablespoon cocoa nibs
- 1 and ½ tablespoon coconut oil
- 2 tablespoons ghee, melted
  For the filling:
- 4 avocados pitted and peeled
- 5 ounces coconut oil
- 5 ounces cocoa powder
- 2 tablespoons stevia
- 1 tablespoon vanilla extract

Directions:
1. In your food processor mix apricots with chia seeds, cocoa nibs, 1 and ½ tablespoons oil and ghee, blend well and spread on the bottom of a cake pan.
2. In your blender, mix the avocados with 5 ounces coconut oil, cocoa, stevia and vanilla, blend well, spread over the cake base, introduce in the fridge for 4 hours, slice and serve.
   Enjoy!

Nutritional Value per serving: calories 181, fat 2, fiber 2, carbs 10, protein 7

176. Cashew and Blueberries Cake
Preparation time: 5 hours
Cooking time: 0 minutes
Servings: 6

Ingredients:
  For the crust:
- ½ cup dates, pitted
- 1 tablespoon water
- ½ teaspoon vanilla

- ½ cup almonds, chopped
  For the cake:
- 2 and ½ cups cashews soaked for 8 hours and drained
- 1 cup blueberries
- ¾ cup stevia
- 1 tablespoon coconut oil

Directions:
1. In your food processor, mix dates with water, vanilla and almonds pulse well and press on the bottom of a cake pan.
2. In your blender, mix stevia with coconut oil, cashews and blueberries, blend well, spread over the crust, and keep in the freezer for 5 hours, slice and serve.
   Enjoy!

Nutritional Value per serving: calories 200, fat 0.5, fiber 4, carbs 12, protein 4

177. Mandarin, Carrots and Dates Cake
Preparation time: 3 hours
Cooking time: 0 minutes
Servings: 6

Ingredients:
- 3 carrots, peeled and grated
- 1/3 cup dates, pitted
- 4 mandarins, peeled
- A handful walnuts, soaked for 5 hours and drained
- 8 tablespoons coconut oil
- 1 cup cashews
- Juice of 2 lemons
- 2 tablespoons stevia

Directions:
1. In your food processor, mix carrots with dates, walnuts, mandarins and half of the coconut oil, blend very well and spread on the bottom of a cake pan.
2. In your blender, combine the walnuts with lemon juice, the rest of the oil and stevia, blend, spread over the carrot mix, and keep in the fridge for 3 hours, slice and serve.
Enjoy!

Nutritional Value per serving: calories 200, fat 2, fiber 4, carbs 10, protein 4

178. Creamy Coconut and Green Tea Pudding

Preparation time: 10 minutes
Cooking time: 2 minutes
Servings: 6

Ingredients:
- 14 ounces coconut milk
- 2 tablespoons green tea powder
- 14 ounces coconut cream
- 3 tablespoons stevia

Directions:
1. Put the milk in a pan, add stevia and green tea powder, stir, bring to a simmer, cook for 2 minutes, cool down, add the coconut cream, stir, divide into bowls and serve cold.
Enjoy!

Nutritional Value per serving: calories 180, fat 3, fiber 3, carbs 7, protein 5

179.   Nut Balls
Preparation time: 30 minutes
Cooking time: 0 minute
Servings: 4

Ingredients:
- 10 hazelnuts, roasted
- 1 cup hazelnuts, roasted and chopped
- 1 teaspoon vanilla extract
- 2 tablespoons cocoa powder
- ¼ cup stevia

Directions:
1. Put 1 cup chopped hazelnuts in your food processor, blend, add vanilla extract, cocoa powder and stevia, blend again well and put in a bowl.
2. Roll the 10 hazelnuts in cocoa hazelnut powder mix, introduce in the freezer for 20 minutes and serve.
Enjoy!

Nutritional value: calories 97, fat 2, fiber 2, carbs 11, protein 2

180.   Almond Chocolate Cookies
Prep Time: 25 MINServe: 12)

Ingredients:
2 cups almond meal
1 1/2 tsp almond extract
4 Tbsp cocoa powder
5 Tbsp coconut oil, melted
2 Tbsp almond milk
4 Tbsp agave nectar
2 tsp vanilla extract
1/8 tsp baking soda
1/8 tsp salt

Directions:
1. Preheat oven to 340F degrees.
2. In a deep bowl mix salt, cocoa powder, almond meal and baking soda.
3. In a separate bowl, whisk together melted coconut oil, almond milk, almond and vanilla extract and maple syrup. Merge the almond meal mixture with almond milk mixture and mix well.
4. In a greased baking pan pour the batter evenly. Bake for 10-15 minutes. 5. Once ready let cool on a wire rack and serve.

Nutritional Value per serving: Calories 79.32 Total Fats 5.94g Net Carbs: 7.2g Protein 0.46g Fiber 0.61G)

181. Carrot Flowers Muffins

Prep Time: 50 MINServe: 12

-

Ingredients:
2 eggs
2 cups shredded carrots
1/4 cup coconut flour
1/2 cup coconut oil
1 tsp vanilla extract
1/4 cup Erythritol
2 tsp ground cinnamon
1 tsp baking powder

Directions:
1. Preheat oven to 350F. PrePARE12 muffin tins.
2. In your food processor, add in carrots, eggs, coconut oil, Erythritol, and vanilla. Blend together until combined.
3. In a separate bowl, mix together coconut flour, cinnamon, and baking powder.
4. Pour the carrot mixture into the dry ingredients and mix until completely combined.
5. Pour carrot mixture into the muffin tin and bake for about 30-35 minutes.
6. Remove from the oven, and let cool for at least 30 minutes. Serve.

182. Nutritional Value per serving: Calories 127.55 Apple Pumpkin Cookies

Preparation time: 10 minutes
Cooking time: 20 minutes
Servings: 4

Ingredients:
- ¼ cup apple juice
- 1 and ½ cup pumpkin puree
- 1 teaspoon vanilla extract
- ¼ cup coconut milk
- 1 cup almond milk
- ½ cup coconut flour

Directions:
1. In a bowl, mix apple juice with pumpkin puree, vanilla extract, coconut milk, add almond meal and coconut flour and stir well.
2. Drop spoonfuls of batter on a lined baking sheet, flatten, introduce in the oven at 350 degrees F, bake for 25 minutes and serve cold.
Enjoy!

Nutritional Value per serving: calories 140, fat 7, fiber 2, carbs 12, protein 10

183.   Peppermint Chocolate Ice Cream
Prep Time: 35 MINServe: 3

Ingredients:
1/2 tsp Peppermint extract
1 cup heavy cream
1 cup cheese cream
1 tsp pure vanilla extract
1 tsp Liquid Stevia extract
100% Dark Chocolate for topping

Directions:
1. Place ice cream bowl in the freezer.
2. In a metal bowl, add all ingredients except chocolate and whisk well.
3. Put back in the freezer for 5 minutes.
4. **Set up ice cream maker and add liquid.**
5. Before serving, top the ice cream with chocolate shavings. Serve.

Nutritional Value per serving: Calories 286.66 Total Fats 29.96g Net Carbs: 2.7G Protein 2.6G

184.   Puff-up Coconut Waffles
Prep Time: 20 MINServe: 8

Ingredients:
1 cup coconut flour
1/2 cup heavy (whipping) cream
5 eggs
1/4 tsp pink salt
1/4 tsp baking soda
1/4 cup coconut milk
2 tsp Yacon Syrup
2 Tbsp coconut oil (melted)

Directions:
1. In a large bowl add the eggs and beat with an electric hand mixer for 30 seconds.
2. Add the heavy (whipping) cream and coconut oil into the eggs while you are still mixing. Add the coconut milk, coconut flour, pink salt and baking soda. Mix with the hand mixer for 45 seconds on low speed. Set aside.
3. Heat up your waffle maker well and make the waffles according to your manufactures specifications.
4. Serve hot.

Nutritional Value per serving: Calories 169.21 Total Fats 12.6G Net Carbs: 9.97g Protein 4.39g
    Fiber 0.45g

185.   Raspberry Chocolate Cream
Prep Time: 15 MINServe: 4

Ingredients:
1/2 cup 100% dark chocolate, chopped
1/4 cup of heavy cream
1/2 cup cream cheese, softened

2 Tbsp sugar-free Raspberry Syrup
1/4 cup Erythritol

Directions:
1. In a double boiler melt chopped chocolate and the cream cheese. Add the Erythritol sweetener and continue to stir. Remove from heat, let cool and set aside.
2. When the cream has cooled add in heavy cream and Raspberry syrup and stir well.
3. Pour cream in a bowls or glasses and serve. Keep refrigerated.

Nutritional Value per serving: Calories 157.67 Total Fats 13.51G Net Carbs: 7.47g Protein 1.95g Fiber 1G

186.   Raw Cacao Hazelnut Cookies
Prep Time: 6 HRServe: 24

Ingredients:
2 cups almond flour
1 cup chopped hazelnuts
1/2 cup cacao powder
1/2 cup ground flax
3 Tbsp coconut oil (melted)
1/3 cup water
1/3 cup Erythritol
1/4 tsp liquid Stevia

Directions:
1. In a bowl, mix flax and almond flour, cacao powder.
2. Stir in oil, water, agave, and vanilla. When it is well combined, stir in chopped hazelnuts.
3. Form into balls, press flat with palms and place on dehydrator screens.
4. **Dehydrate one hour at 145, then reduce to 116 and dehydrate for at least five hours.**
5. Serve and enjoy.

Nutritional Value per serving: Calories 181.12 Total Fats 15.69G Net Carbs: 8.75g Protein 4.46g Fiber: 3.45 g

187.   Sinless Pumpkin Cheesecake Muffins
Prep Time: 15 MINServe: 6

Ingredients:
1/2 cup pureed pumpkin
1 tsp pumpkin pie spice
1/2 cup pecans, finely ground
1/2 cup cream cheese
1 Tbsp coconut oil
1/2 tsp pure vanilla extract
1/4 tsp pure Yacon Syrup or Erythritol

Directions:
1. Prepare a muffin tin with liners.
2. Place a few ground pecans into every muffin tin and make a thin crust.

3. In a bowl, blend sweetener, spices, vanilla, coconut and the pumpkin puree. Add in the cream cheese and beat until the mixture is well combined.
4. **Scoop about two tbsp of filling mixture on top of each crust, and smooth the edges.**
5. Pop in the freezer for about 45 minutes.
6. Remove from the muffin tin and let sit for 10 minutes. Serve.

Nutritional Value per serving: Calories 157.34 Total Fats 15.52G Net Carbs: 3.94g Protein 2.22g Fiber: 1.51G

188.   Sour Hazelnuts Biscuits with Arrowroot Tea
Prep Time: 50 MINServe: 12

Ingredients:
1 egg
1/2 cup hazelnuts
3 Tbsp of coconut oil
2 cups almond flour
2 Tbsp of arrowroot tea
2 tsp ginger
1 Tbsp cocoa powder
1/2 cup grapefruit juice
1 orange peel from a half orange
1/2 tsp baking soda
1 pinch of salt

Directions:
1. Preheat oven to 360 F.
2. Make arrowroot tea and let it cool.
3. In a food processor blend the hazelnuts. Add the remaining ingredients and continue blending until mixed well. With your hands form cookies with the batter.
4. **Put the cookies on baking parchment paper, and bake for 30-35 minutes. When ready, remove the tray from the oven and let cool.**
5. Serve warm or cold.

Nutritional Value per serving: Calories 224.08 Total Fats 20.17G Net Carbs: 8.06g Protein 6.36g Fiber 3.25 g

189.   Tartar Keto Cookies
Prep Time: 35 MINServe: 8

Ingredients:
3 eggs
1/8 tsp cream of tartar
1/3 cup cream cheese
1/8 tsp salt
Some oil for greasing

Directions:
1. Preheat oven to 300 F.
2. Line the cookie sheet with parchment paper and grease with some oil.
3. Separate eggs from the egg yolks. Set both in different mixing bowls.

4. **With an electric hand mixer, start beating the egg whites until super bubbly. Add in cream of tartar and beat until stiff peaks form.**
5. In the egg yolk bowl, add in cream cheese and some salt. Beat until the egg yolks are pale yellow.
6. Merge the egg whites into the cream cheese mixture. Stir well.
7. Make cookies and place on the cookie sheet.
8. Bake for about 30-40 minutes. When ready, let them cool on a wire rack and serve.

Nutritional Value per serving: Calories 59.99 Total Fats 5.09g Net Carbs: 0.56g Protein 2.93G

190.   Wild Strawberries Ice Cream
Prep Time: 5 MINServe: 4

Ingredients:
1/2 cup wild strawberries
1/3 cup cream cheese
1 cup heavy cream
1 Tbsp lemon juice
1 tsp pure vanilla extract
1/3 cup of your favorite sweetener
Ice cubes

Directions:
1. Place all ingredients in a blender. Blend until all incorporate well.
2. Refrigerate for 2-3 hour before serving.

Nutritional Value per serving: Calories 176.43 Total Fats 17.69g Net Carbs: 3.37g Protein 1.9g Fiber 0.39g

191.   Mini Lemon Cheesecakes
Prep Time: 5 MINServe: 6

Ingredients:
1 tbsp lemon zest, grated
1 tsp lemon juice
½ tsp stevia powder or (Truvia)
1/4 cup coconut oil, softened
4 tbsp unsalted butter, softened
4 ounces cream cheese (heavy cream)

Directions:
1. Blend all ingredients together with a hand mixer or blender until smooth and creamy.
2. Prepare a cupcake or muffin tin with 6 paper liners.
3. Pour mixture into prepared tin and place in freezer for 2-3 hours or until firm.
4. Sprinkle cups with additional lemon zest. Or try using chopped nuts or shredded, unsweetened coconut.

Nutritional Value per serving: Calories 213 Total Fats 23g Net Carbs: 0.7g Protein 1.5G Fiber: 0.1 g

192.   Chocolate Layered Coconut Cups
Prep Time: 55 MINServe: 10

Ingredients:
Bottom Layer:
1/2 cup unsweetened, shredded coconut
3 tbsp powdered sweeteners such as Splenda or Truvia
1/2 cup coconut butter
1/2 cup coconut oil

Top Layer:
1 1/2 ounces cocoa butter
1-ounce unsweetened chocolate
1/4 cup cocoa powder
1/2 tsp vanilla extract
1/4 cup powdered sweetener such as Splenda or Truvia

Directions:
1. Prepare a mini-muffin pan with 20 mini paper liners.
2. For the bottom layer:
3. Combine coconut oil and coconut butter in a small saucepan over low heat.
4. **Stir until smooth and melted then add the shredded coconut and powdered sweetener until well combined.**
5. Divide the mixture among prepared mini muffin cups and place in the refrigerator for 30 minutes.
6. For the top layer:
7. Combine cocoa butter and unsweetened chocolate together in double boiler or a bowl set over a pan of simmering water. Stir until melted.
8. Stir in the powdered sweetener, then the cocoa powder and mix until smooth.
9. Remove from heat and stir in the vanilla extract.
10. Spoon chocolate mixture over coconut candies and let them set for 15 minutes.
11. Serve and enjoy.

Nutritional Value per serving: Calories 300Total Fats 27g Net Carbs: 14.5G Protein 2G Fiber: 3.9g

193.   Pumpkin Pie Chocolate Cups
Prep Time: 45 MINServe: 18

Ingredients:
For the crust:
3.5 ounces extra dark chocolate - 85% cocoa solids or more
2 tbsp coconut oil

For the pie:
½ cup coconut butter
¼ cup coconut oil
2 tsp pumpkin pie spice mix
½ cup unsweetened pumpkin puree
2 tbsp healthy low-carb sweetener
Optional: 15-20 drops liquid stevia for added sweetness

Directions:
1. Place the chocolate and coconut oil in a double boiler or a glass bowl on top of a small saucepan filled with simmering water. Once completely melted, remove from the heat and set aside.

2. Prepare a mini muffin tin with 18 paper liners.
3. Fill each of the 18 mini muffin cups with 2 tsp of the chocolate mixture.
4. **Place the chocolate in the refrigerator for 10 minutes.**
5. Place the coconut butter, coconut oil, sweetener and pumpkin spice mix into a bowl and melt just like you did the chocolate.
6. Add the pumpkin puree and mix until smooth and well combined.
7. Remove the muffin cupsfrom the fridge and add a heaping tsp of the pumpkin & coconut mixture into every cup.
8. Place back in the refrigerator and let it sit for 30 minutes.
9. When done, keep refrigerated. Coconut oil and butter get very soft at room temperature.
10. Store in the refrigerator.
11. Serve and enjoy.

Nutritional Value per serving: Calories 92Total Fats 9.1G Net Carbs: 3.4g Protein 0.7g Fiber: 1.6G

194.   Chocolate Pecan Bites
Prep Time: 3 HRServe: 12

Ingredients:
2 oz 100% dark chocolate
2.5 oz pecan halves
Cinnamon
Nutmeg

Directions:
1. Preheat oven to 350 F.
2. Place the pecan halves on a parchment paper and bake in the oven for 6-7 minutes. When ready, let cool and set aside.
3. Melt the dark chocolate.
4. Dip each pecan half in the melted dark chocolate and place back on the parchment paper.
5. Sprinkle a cinnamon and nutmeg on top of the chocolate covered pecans.
6. Before serving place in refrigerator for 2-3 hours.

Nutritional Value per serving: Calories 52.13 Total Fats 4.96g Net Carbs: 2.32G Protein 0.64g |Fiber: 0.71G

195.   Hazelnuts Chocolate Cream
Prep Time: 5 MINServe: 4

Ingredients:
1 cup hazelnuts halves
4 Tbsp unsweetened cocoa powder
1 tsp pure vanilla extract
2 Tbsp coconut oil
4 Tbsp granulated Stevia (or sweetener of choice)

Directions:
1. Place all the ingredients in your blender. Blend until smooth well.
2. Store in the fridge for 1 hour. Serve and enjoy!

Nutritional Value per serving: Calories 302.88 Total Fats 29.65g Net Carbs: 9.5g Protein 6.39g Fiber 5.12G

196.   Instant Coffee Ice Cream
Prep Time: 20 MINServe: 2

Ingredients:
1 Tbsp Instant Coffee
2 Tbsp Cocoa Powder
1 cup coconut milk
1/4 cup heavy cream
1/4 tsp flax seeds
2 Tbsp Erythritol
15 drops liquid Nutria

Directions:
1. Add all ingredients except the flax seeds into a container of your immersion blender.
2. Blend well until all ingredients are incorporated well. Slowly add in flax seeds until a slightly thicker mixture is formed. Add the mass to your ice cream machine and follow manufacturer's instructions.
3. Ready! Serve!

Nutritional Value per serving: Calories 286.99 Total Fats 29.21G Net Carbs: 9.39g Protein 3.18G Fiber: 1.88 g

197.   Jam "Eye" Cookies
Prep Time: 36 MINServe: 16

Ingredients:
2 eggs
1 cup almond flour
2 Tbsp coconut flour
2 Tbsp sugar-free jam per taste
1/2 cup natural sweetener
4 tbsp coconut oil
1/2 tsp pure vanilla extract
1/2 tsp almond extract
1 tbsp shredded coconut
1/2 tsp baking powder
1/4 tsp cinnamon
1/2 tsp salt

Directions:
1. Preheat your oven to 350 F. In a big bowl, combine all your dry ingredients and whisk.
2. Add in your wet ingredients and combine well using a hand mixer or a whisk.
3. With your hand for making the patties and place the cookies on a parchment paper-lined baking sheet. Using your finger make an indent in the middle of each cookie.
4. Bake for about 16 minutes or until the cookies turn golden.
5. Once ready, let the cookies cool on a wire rack and fill each indent with sugar-free jam.
6. Before serving sprinkle some shredded coconut on top of each cookie. Enjoy!

Nutritional Value per serving: Calories 95.1 Total Fats 8.61G Net Carbs: 2.79G Protein 2.71G Fiber 1.2G

198.   Lemon Coconut Pearls
Prep Time: 15 MINServe: 4

Ingredients:
3 packages of True Lemon (Crystallized Citrus for Water)
1/4 cup shredded coconut, unsweetened
1 cup cream cheese
1/4 cup granulated Stevia

Directions:
1. In a bowl, combine cream cheese, lemon, and Stevia. Blend well until incorporated.
2. Once the mixture is well combined, put it back in the fridge to harden up a bit.
3. Roll into 16 balls and dip each ball into shredded coconut. Refrigerate for several hours. Serve.

Nutritional Value per serving: Calories 216.06 Total Fats 21.53G Net Carbs: 3.12G Protein 3.61G Fiber 0.45g

199.   Lime & Vanilla Cheesecake
Prep Time: 2 HR 5 MINServe: 2

Ingredients:
1/4 cup cream cheese, softened
2 Tbsp heavy cream
1 tsp lime juice
1 egg
1 tsp pure vanilla extract
2-4 Tbsp Erythritol or Stevia

Directions:
1. In a microwave-safe bowl combine all ingredients. Place in a microwave and cook on HIGH for 90 seconds.
2. Every 30 seconds stir to combine the ingredients well.
3. Transfer mixture to a bowl and refrigerate for at least 2 hours.
4. Before serving top with whipped cream or coconut powder.

Nutritional Value per serving: Calories 140.42 Total Fats 13.04G Net Carbs: 1.38G Protein 4.34g Fiber 0.01G

200.   Mouse of Chocolate
Prep Time: 15 MINServe: 4

Ingredients:
1/4 cup of heavy cream
1 1/4 cup coconut cream
2 Tbsp of cocoa powder
3 Tbsp of Erythritol (or Stevia)
1 Tbsp pure vanilla essence

Shredded coconut, unsweetened

Directions:
1. Add coconut cream and heavy cream in the bowl and combine together using a hand mixer on low speed.
2. Add the remaining ingredients and mix on low speed for 2-3 minutes until the mix is thick.
3. Serve in individual ramekins sprinkled with unsweetened shredded coconut.

Nutritional Value per serving: Calories 305.19 Total Fats 31.91G Net Carbs: 6.97g Protein 3.56g
Fiber 2.55G

201.   Strawberry Pudding
Prep Time: 35 MINServe: 3

Ingredients:
4 egg yolks
2 Tbsp butter
1/4 cup coconut flour
2 Tbsp heavy cream
1/4 cup strawberries
1/4 tsp baking powder
2 Tbsp coconut oil
2 tsp lemon juice
Zest 1 Lemon
2 Tbsp Erythritol
10 drops Liquid Stevia

Directions:
1. Preheat oven to 350 F.
2. In a bowl beat the egg yolks with electric mixer until they're pale in color. Add in Erythritol and 10 drops liquid Stevia. Beat again until fully combined.
3. Add in heavy cream, lemon juice, and the zest of 1 lemon. Add the coconut and butter. Beat well until no lumps are found.
4. Sift the dry ingredients over the wet ingredients, and then mix well on a slow speed.
5. Distribute the strawberries evenly in the batter by pushing them into the top of the batter.
6. Bake for 20-25 minutes. Once finished, let cool for 5 minutes and serve.

Nutritional Value per serving: Calories 258.65 Total Fats 23.46G Net Carbs: 9.3g Protein 3.98g
Fiber 0.61G

202.   Kiwi Fiend Ice Cream
Prep Time: 8 HR 15 MINServe: 6

Ingredients:
3 egg yolks
1 1/2 cup Kiwi, pureed
1 cup heavy cream
1/3 cup Erythritol
1/2 tsp pure vanilla extract
1/8 tsp chia seeds

Directions:
1. In a saucepan heat up the heavy cream. Add erythritol and simmer until the erythritol has dissolved.
2. Beat 3 egg yolks in a medium sized mixing bowl with an electric mixer. Add in hot cream mixture, 1 tsp at a time to the eggs while beating. Add in some pure vanilla extract and mix. Add in 1/8 tsp. of chia seeds.
3. Once the ingredients are combined, put your bowl into the freezer and let it chill for 1-2 hours, stirring twice.
4. In a meanwhile puree the kiwi no more than 1-2 seconds. When the ice cream is getting a thicker, about 1 hour in add the kiwi mixture to the cream and mix well.
5. Let the kiwi ice cream to chill at least 6-8 hours. Serve in chilled glasses.

Nutritional Value per serving: Calories 192.47 Total Fats 17.2G Net Carbs: 8.13G Protein 2.69g Fiber 1.46G

203.   Minty Avocado Lime Sorbet
Prep Time: 3 HR 15 MINServe: 6

Ingredients:
1 cup coconut milk
2 avocados, sliced vertically into 5 pieces
1/4 mint leaves, chopped
1/4 cup powdered Erythritol
2 limes, juiced
1/4 tsp liquid Stevia

Directions:
1. Place avocado pieces on foil and squeeze the ½ lime juice over the tops.
2. Place avocado in the freezer for at least 3 hours.
3. Using a spice grinder, powder Erythritol.
4. In a pan, bring coconut milk to a boil.
5. Zest the 2 limes you have while coconut milk is heating up. Add lime zest and continue to let the milk reduce in volume.
6. Remove and place the coconut milk into a container and store in the freezer.
7. Chop mint leaves. Remove avocados from the freezer.
8. Add avocado, mint leaves, and juice from lime into the food processor. Pulse until a chunky consistency is achieved.
9. Pour coconut milk mixture over the avocados in the food processor. Add Liquid Stevia to this.
10. Pulse mixture together about 2-3 minutes.
11. Return to freezer to freeze, or serve immediately!

Nutritional Value per serving: Calories 184.18 Total Fats 17.26G Net Carbs: 9.65g Protein 1.95G Fiber 4.59g

204.   Morning Zephyr Cake
Prep Time: 40 MINServe: 8

Ingredients:
3 Tbsp coconut oil
2 Tbsp grounded flax seeds

8 Tbsp almonds, grounded
1 cup Greek Yogurt
1 Tbsp cocoa powder for dusting
1 cup heavy whipping cream
1 tsp Baking Powder
1 tsp Baking Soda
1 tsp pure vanilla essence
1 pinch pink salt
1 cup Stevia or Erythritol sweetener

Directions:
1. Pre-heat the oven to 350 F degrees.
2. In the blender first add the grounded almonds, grounded flax seeds, and the baking powder and soda. Blend for a minute.
3. Add the salt, coconut oil and blend some more. Add the sweetener and blend for 2-3 minutes.
4. Add the Greek yogurt and blend for a minute or so, until a fine consistency is reached.
5. Take out the batter in a bowl and add the vanilla essence, and mix with a light hand.
6. Grease the baking dish and drop the batter in it.
7. Bake for 30 minutes. Let cool on a wire rack. Serve.

Nutritional Value per serving: Calories 199.84 Total Fats 20.69G Net Carbs: 3.22G Protein 2.56g Fiber 1.17g

205.   Peanut Butter Balls
Prep Time: 22 MINServe: 16

Ingredients:
2 eggs
2 1/2 cup of peanut butter
1/2 cup shredded coconut (unsweetened)
1/2 cup of Xylitol
1 Tbsp of pure vanilla extract

Directions:
1. Preheat oven to 320 F.
2. Mix all ingredients together by your hands.
3. After the ingredients are thoroughly mixed, roll into heaped tbsp sized balls and press into a baking tray lined with baking paper.
4. Bake in preheated oven for 12 minutes.
5. When ready, let cool on a wire rack.
6. Serve and enjoy.

Nutritional Value per serving: Calories 254.83 Total Fats 21.75G Net Carbs: 8.31G Protein 10.98G Fiber 2.64G

206.   Pecan Flax Seed Blondies
Prep Time: 40 MINServe: 16

Ingredients:
3 eggs

2 1/4 cups pecans, roasted
3 Tbsp heavy cream
1 Tbsp salted caramel syrup
1/2 cup flax seeds, ground
1/4 cup butter, melted
1/4 cup erythritol, powdered
10 drops Liquid Stevia
1 tsp baking powder
1 pinch salt

Directions:
1. Preheat oven to 350F.
2. In a baking pan roast pecans for 10 minutes.
3. Grind 1/2 cup flax seeds in a spice grinder. Place flax seed powder in a bowl. Grind Erythritol in a spice grinder until powdered. Set in the same bowl as the flax seed meal.
4. Place 2/3 of roasted pecans in food processor and process until a smooth nut butter is formed.
5. Add eggs, liquid Stevia, salted caramel syrup, and a pinch of salt to the flax seed mixture. Mix well. Add pecan butter to the batter and mix again.
6. Crush the remaining roasted pecans into chunks.
7. Add crushed pecans and 1/4 cup melted butter into the batter.
8. Mix batter well and then add heavy cream and baking powder. Mix everything together well.
9. Place the batter into baking tray and bake for 20 minutes.
10. Let cool for about 10 minutes.
11. Cut into square and serve.

Nutritional Value per serving: Calories 180.45 Total Fats 18.23G Net Carbs: 3.54g Protein 3.07g Fiber 1.78G

207. Lemonita Granita

Serves: 10
Preparation: 10 minutes

Ingredients

4 fresh lemons, juice about 3/4 cup
1 ½ cups of natural sweetener (Stevia, Erythritol...etc.)
3 cups water
2 lemon peeled, pulp

Directions

1. In a saucepan, heat all ingredients over medium heat.
2. Remove from heat, and let cool on room temperature.
3. Pour the mixture in a baking dish, wrap with plastic membrane and freeze for 6 - 8 hours.
4. Remove granita from the freezer, scratch with big fork and stir.
5. Serve in chilled glasses and enjoy!
6. Keep in freezer.

Nutrition information:
Calories: 13 Carbohydrates: 3g Proteins: 1g Fat: 1g Fiber: 0.2g

208.　Low Carb Blackberry Ice Cream

Serves: 8
Preparation: 10 minutes

Ingredients

3/4 lb of frozen blackberries, unsweetened
1 1/4 cup of caned coconut milk
1/4 cup of granulated erythritol sweetener or to taste
2 Tbsp of almond flour
1 pinch of ground vanilla
1 Tbsp of MCT oil

Directions

1. Put all the ingredients in a blender. Make sure blackberries are still frozen.
2. Blend until a creamy, homogeneous mass is formed.
3. Pour the blackberry mixture in a container and freeze overnight.
4. Serve in chilled glasses or bowls.

Nutrition information:
Calories: 83 Carbohydrates: 5g Proteins: 1g Fat: 8g Fiber: 2.5g

209.　Murky Coconut Ice Cream

Serves: 8
Preparation: 15 minutes

Ingredients

2 can (11 oz) of frozen coconut milk
2 scoop powdered chocolate protein
4 Tbsp of stevia sweetener
2 Tbsp of cocoa powder

Directions

1. In a high-speed blender, stir the iced coconut milk.
2. Blend for 30 - 45 seconds and then add the remaining ingredients.
3. Blend again until get a thick cream.
4. Pour the mixture in a container and store in freezer for 4 hours.
5. To prevent forming ice crystals, beat the mixture every 30 minutes.
6. Ready! Serve in chilled glasses.

Nutrition information:
Calories: 135 Carbohydrates: 3g Proteins: 4g Fat: 15g Fiber: 1g

210.   Peppermint Chocolate Popsicles

Serves: 8
Preparation: 20 minutes

Ingredients

3 cups coconut milk (canned), divided
2 gelatin sheets
3 cup packed peppermint leaves
1 cup stevia granulate sweetener
1/4 tsp pure peppermint extract
3/4 cup of dark chocolate (60- 69% of cacao solid) melted

Directions

1. Soak gelatin in a little coconut milk for 10 minutes.
2. In a saucepan, heat the coconut milk and peppermint leaves; cook for 3 minutes stirring constantly.
3. Add soaked gelatin and stir until completely dissolved.
4. Remove the saucepan from heat, cover and set aside for 20 - 25 minutes.
5. Strain the mint mixture through a colander into the bowl, and add the stevia sweetener: stir well. Pour the peppermint extract and stir.
6. Place bowl in the freezer for about one hour.
7. Remove from freezer and stir melted dark chocolate.
8. Pour into Popsicle molds, insert sticks in each mold, and freeze overnight.
9. Remove popsicles from the mold and serve.

Nutrition information:
Calories: 231 Carbohydrates: 8g Proteins: 3g Fat: 22g Fiber: 1g

211.   Perfect Strawberry Ice Cream

Serves: 12
Preparation: 20 minutes

Ingredients

2 lbs of strawberries
2 1/4 cups of water
2 Tbsp of coconut butter, softened
1 1/2 cups of natural granulated sweetener (Stevia, Truvia, Erythritol...etc.)
2 egg whites
1 lemon squeezed

Directions

1. Heat strawberries, water, coconut butter and stevia sweetener in a saucepan over medium-low heat.
2. When strawberries softened, remove the saucepan from heat, and allow it to cool on room temperature.
3. Whisk the egg whites until stiff; add the lemon juice and stir.
4. Add the egg whites mixture to strawberry mixture and gently stir with wooden spatula.
5. Refrigerate the ice cream mixture for 2 hours.
6. Pour cold ice cream mixture into ice cream maker, turn on the machine, and do according to manufacturer's directions.
7. In the case that you do not have ice cream maker, pour the mixture in a container and freeze for 8 hours.

Nutrition information:
Calories: 50 Carbohydrates: 6g Proteins: 1g Fat: 5g Fiber: 2g

212.   Raskolnikov Vanilla Ice Cream

Serves: 8
Preparation: 10 minutes
Cooking: 20 minutes

Ingredients

3 sheets of gelatin sugar-free
2 US pints of cream
1/2 vanilla stick
1/2 cup stevia granulated sweetener
4 egg yolks
3 Tbsp of vodka

Directions

1. Soak gelatin in some water (about 1 cup per 1 sheet of gelatin)
2. Heat the cream in a saucepan along with vanilla seeds and stevia sweetener; stir.
3. Add the egg yolks, and continue to stir for further 2 - 3 minutes.
4. Remove from heat, add gelatin and stir well.
5. Pour vodka and stir again; allow the mixture to cool.
6. Pour the mixture in a container and refrigerate for at least 4 hours.
7. Remove the mixture in an ice cream maker; follow manufacturer's instructions.
8. Or, pour the mixture in a freeze-safe container and freeze overnight.
9. Beat every 45 minutes with the mixture to prevent ice crystallization.
10. Serve and enjoy!

Nutrition information:
Calories: 118 Carbohydrates: 4g Proteins: 3g Fat: 10g Fiber: 0g

213.   Traditional Spanish Cold Cream with Walnuts

Serves: 6
Preparation: 5 minutes
Cooking: 3 hours

Ingredients

3 cups of almond milk
3 cups of liquid cream
1 cup of ground walnuts
3/4 cup of natural sweetener (Stevia, Erythritol...etc.) or to taste
1 cinnamon stick

Directions

1. Add all ingredients from the list above in your Slow Cooker.
2. Cover and cook on HIGH for 3 hours.
3. During cooking, stir several times with wooden spoon.
4. If your cream is too dense, add more almond milk.
5. Store cream in glass container and refrigerate for 4 hours.
6. Remove cream from the refrigerator 15 minutes before serving.

   Nutrition information:
Calories: 193 Carbohydrates: 5g Proteins: 8g Fat: 20g Fiber: 2g

214.   Sinless Chocolate Ice Cream

Serves: 6
Preparation: 15 minutes

Ingredients

1 can (15 oz) coconut milk
1/2 cup cocoa powder
1/4 cup natural sweetener (Stevia, Truvia, Erythritol...etc.)
1 tsp vanilla extract
Chopped nuts or shredded coconut for serving (optional)

Directions

1. Combine all ingredients in a bowl.
2. Use an electric mixer and beat the mixture until all ingredients combine well.
3. Transfer the mixture in a freezer-safe bowl and freeze for 4 hours.
4. To prevent ice crystallization, beat the ice cream with the mixer every hour.
5. Serve garnished with sliced nuts or shredded coconuts.

   Nutrition information:

Calories: 204 Carbohydrates: 7g Proteins: 4g Fat: 21g Fiber: 4.5g

215.   True Cinnamon Ice Cream

Serves: 8
Preparation: 10 minutes
Cooking:15 minutes

Ingredients

1 1/2 cup almond milk (or coconut milk)
1 cinnamon stick
1 1/2 cup natural granulated sweetener (Stevia, Truvia, Erythritol...etc.)
1 1/2 Tbsp lemon peel
8 egg yolks from free-range chicken
1 pinch of salt
1 1/2 Tbsp ground cinnamon
1 cup cream

Directions

1. In a saucepan, heat almond milk, cinnamon stick, stevia sweetener and lemon peel.
2. Bring to boil, reduce the heat and stir over low heat for 10 minutes,
3. In a bowl, beat the egg yolks with the pinch of salt until frothy. Place the egg mixture in a glass bowl over the bain marie, and stir until thicken.
4. Remove the cinnamon stick and lemon peel, pour the almond milk in egg yolk mixture; continue to until the mixture becomes thick.
5. Remove the mixture from heat, add ground cinnamon, stir; set aside and allow it to cool on room temperature.
6. In a bowl, beat the cream until double in volume.
7. Combine the cream with egg mixture and gently stir with wooden spatula.
8. Place the ice cream in the freezer until frozen or for at least 6-8 hours.
9. Serve and enjoy!

        Nutrition information:
Calories: 181 Carbohydrates: 6g Proteins: 4g Fat: 17g Fiber: 2g

216.   Vanilla Coconut Ice Cream

Serves: 8
Preparation: 10 minutes

Ingredients

15 oz of coconut cream
2 Tbsp of coconut butter, softened
1/2 cup of stevia sweetener or to taste

1 pinch of salt
2 tsp vanilla extract
1 tsp vanilla powder

Directions

1. Place all ingredients to the mixing bowl and beat for 3 - 4 minutes.
2. Pour the mixture in a container, cover with membrane and freeze for 4 - 5 hours.
3. After one hour, remove the mixture, place in a mixing bowl and beat it again for 3 - 4 minutes.
4. Repeat this process every half an hour in order to get smooth ice cream without the ice crystals.
5. When done, serve the ice cream in chilled bowls or glasses and serve.

Nutrition information:
Calories: 210 Carbohydrates: 3g Proteins: 3g Fat: 7g Fiber: 2g

217.   Whole Coconut Ice Cream

Serves: 10
Preparation: 10 minutes

Ingredients

4 cups of coconut cream or full-fat coconut milk
2 Tbsp of coconut aminos
2 Tbsp of coconut extract
1/2 cup of natural sweetener stevia or to taste
1/2 cup of coconut flakes for serving (optional)

Directions

1. In a large bowl, stir all ingredients.
2. Pour the ice cream mixture in container and freeze for 8 hours.
3. Stir every hour to avoid ice cream crystallization.
4. When done, remove the ice cream from freezer.
5. Serve in chilled glasses and sprinkle with coconut flakes.

Nutrition information:
Calories: 361 Carbohydrates: 6g Proteins: 4g Fat: 37g Fiber: 3g

218.   "Stroganoff" Queso Fresco Cheese

Serves: 4
Preparation: 5 minutes
Cooking: 12 minutes

Ingredients

2 Tbsp of olive oil

1 of chopped green onion
1 cup of fresh button mushrooms
1 grated tomato
1 lb of Queso fresco- cheese cut into cubes
1 cup of fresh cream
Salt to taste
Worcestershire sauce to taste
Mustard (Dijon, English, ground stone) to taste
Ketchup to taste

Directions

1. Heat the oil in a large skillet and sauté the onion until soft.
2. Add mushrooms and gently stir for 2 - 3 minutes.
3. Add grated tomato, and season with the salt, Worcestershire sauce, ketchup and mustard.
4. Bring to boil; add cheese cubes and stir well.
5. Cook just for one minute, to avoid the cheese melting.
6. Add the fresh cream and stir.
7. Remove from the heat, and allow it to cool for 5 minutes.
8. Serve.

Nutrition information:
Calories: 469 Carbohydrates: 5.7g Proteins: 19.5g Fat: 48g Fiber: 0.7g

219.   Courgettes with Goat Cheese Cake

Serves: 4
Preparation: 15 minutes
Cooking: 2 hours

Ingredients

Non-stick cooking spray for greasing
6 courgettes/zucchini grated
1 handful fresh mint roughly chopped
2 Eggs from free-range chickens
1 Tbsp of almond flour
1/2 tsp of baking soda
3/4 cup goat cheese, crumbled

Directions

1. Grease the bottom and sides of your Crock Pot; set aside.
2. Grate the courgettes/zucchini and squeeze out all the excess water; place in a large bowl.
3. Add eggs, crumbled goat cheese, almond flour, baking soda and mint; stir through.
4. Pour batter in prepared Crock Pot.
5. Cover and cook on LOW for 2 – 3 hours.
6. Allow cake to cool, slice and serve.

Nutrition information:

Calories: 117 Carbohydrates: 2g Proteins: 8g Fat: 10g Fiber: 0.3g

220.   Dark Nutty Chocolate Sauce

Serves: 8
Preparation: 5 minutes
Cooking: 4 hours

Ingredients

4 cups of almond milk
2 cups fresh cream
1 1/2 cups grated dark chocolate (70 - 80% cacao solid)
1 tsp of espresso coffee (two shoots)
2 Tbsp of ground almonds
1/2 tsp of ground cinnamon
Pinch of ground red pepper (optional)
Natural sweetener (Stevia, Truvia, Erythritol...etc.) to taste

Directions

1. Place all ingredients in your Crock Pot.
2. Cover and cook on SLOW for 4 hours or HIGH for 2 hours.
3. Open lid and give a good stir.
4. Allow cream to cool before serving.
5. Keep refrigerated.

        Nutrition information:
Calories: 263 Carbohydrates: 9g Proteins: 3.5g Fat: 22g Fiber: 2g

221.   Irresistible Keto Lemon Cake

Serves: 10
Preparation: 15 minutes
Cooking: 3 hours and 15 minutes

Ingredients

1/3 cup almond butter, melted
2 cups almond flour
3/4 tsp baking soda
1 pinch of salt (optional)
1 cup of natural sweetener (Stevia, Truvia, Erythritol...etc.)
2 Eggs from free-range chickens
3 medium lemons
3 eggs from free-range chickens

Directions

1. Line your Crock Pot with parchment paper.
2. In a bowl, combine the almond flour, sweetener, baking soda and a pinch of salt (optional).
3. In a separate bowl, whisk eggs; add lemon juice and the lemon zest.
4. Combine the flour mixture with egg mixture and stir until all ingredients combined well.
5. Pour the batter into Crock Pot.
6. Cover and cook on LOW setting for 3 - 3 1/2 hours.
7. Transfer cake to the plate, let it cool completely, cut in bars and serve.

Nutrition information:
Calories: 236 Carbohydrates: 6g Proteins: 835g Fat: 22g Fiber: 3g

222.　Keto Blueberry Topping

Serves: 4
Preparation: 10 minutes
Cooking: 2 hours and 15 minutes

Ingredients

3/4 cup natural sweetener (Stevia, Truvia, Erythritol...etc.)
2 Tbsp of water
2 Tbsp of butter
1 cup fresh blueberries (or frozen blueberries)
Juice from 1 lemon
Zest from 1 lemon

Directions

1. Heat the sweetener and water in a saucepan over low heat. Stir approximately 3 to 5 minutes until make nice, smooth syrup.
2. Add fresh butter, and stir to get smooth and shine surface.
3. Add blueberries in your Crock Pot and pour syrup evenly to cover blueberries.
4. Sprinkle the lemon zest, and drizzle with fresh lemon juice; gentle stir.
5. Cover and cook on LOW for 2 hours.
6. Open the lid and give a good stir.
7. Keep refrigerated.

Nutrition information:
Calories: 76 Carbohydrates: 6.5g Proteins: 0.5g Fat: 7g Fiber: 4g

223.　Sinless Raspberries Cake

Serves: 6
Preparation: 15 minutes
Cooking: 2 hours

Ingredients

6 large eggs
1/4 cup natural sweetener (Stevia, Truvia, Erythritol...etc.)
1 tsp cinnamon
1/4 cup olive oil
2 cups fresh raspberries

Directions

1. Line the bottom of your Crock Pot with parchment paper; set aside.
2. Beat eggs with a hand mixer in a bowl; add the sweetener oil and cinnamon.
3. Pour the egg mixture in prepared Crock Pot.
4. Sprinkle the raspberries over the egg mixture evenly.
5. Cover and cook on HIGH for 1 hour and 30 minutes, on LOW for 2 hours and 30 minutes.
6. Remove the cake from the Crock Pot, allow to cool, slice and serve.

Nutrition information:
Calories: 173 Carbohydrates: 5g Proteins: 15g Fat: 7g Fiber: 3g

224.   Strawberry Ocean Sauce

Serves: 12
Preparation: 5 minutes
Cooking: 3 hours

Ingredients

2 lbs. of fresh strawberries
1 1/2 cups natural sweetener (Stevia, Truvia, Erythritol...etc.)
2 Tbsp of vanilla extract
1 1/4 cup water
1/2 lemon juice
2 cinnamon sticks

Directions

1. Place all ingredients in your Slow Cooker and stir well,
2. Cover and cook on LOW for 3 hours.
3. Open lid and give and good stir.
4. Allow sauce to cool completely.
5. Remove cinnamon sticks and store into glass jar; keep refrigerated.

Nutrition information:
Calories: 35 Carbohydrates: 6g Proteins: 1g Fat: 11g Fiber: 1g

Conclusion

Being on a Ketogenic diet will probably be the best decision you will ever take. Once you start this diet, you will soon feel and look amazing.

The Ketogenic diet is the healthiest these days and more and more people opt for it each day. You should become one of millions of people who chose this healthy lifestyle each day.

Overall, the Ketogenic diet will definitely change your life. Its benefits will surprise you for sure and you will end up recommending it to everyone soon enough.

So, don't hesitate too much! Start a Ketogenic diet today and use our exceptional cooking guide to prepare the best Ketogenic meals ever!

Made in the USA
Coppell, TX
16 May 2021

55730420R00066